FAMOUS Friends

Best Buds, Rocky Relationships, and Awesomely Odd Couples from Past to Present

by Jennifer Castle & Bill Spring

SCHOLASTIC INC.

For Peggy, and all the times we were famous in our own minds. —J.C.

For Adam, a best friend through the years and across the miles. —B.S.

Photos ©: cover Jeter and Rodriguez bottom: Peter Morgan PM/GN/Reuters; cover Fitzgerald with Monroe: Bettmann/Getty Images; cover Ella Fitzgerald: Gilles Petard/Getty Images; cover Marilyn Monroe: Evening Standard/Getty Images; cover Jeter and Rodriguez top: Tom DiPace/Getty Images; cover Swift with Lorde bottom: Kevin Mazur/Getty Images; cover Swift with Lorde top: Jon Kopaloff/Getty Images; 1 blackboard texture and throughout: Stillfx/Fotolia; 1 heart and design artwork and throughout: irur/Fotolia; 4 main: Library of Congress; 4 left: Susan Law Cain/iStockphoto; 5 left: WDC Photos/Alamy Images; 5 right: dhimages/Alamy Images; 6-7 signing of Declaration of Independence: Maxim Anisimov/iStockphoto; 6 John Adams: Library of Congress; 6 board: Andrey Kuzmin/Fotolia; 6 quill pen and ink: esolla/Fotolia; 6 Thomas Jefferson: Charles Willson Peale/Alamy Images; 8 top: Susan Law Cain; 8 bottom: sumartin/Fotolia; 9 top: Joe Cicak/iStockphoto; 9 bottom left: traveler1116/iStockphoto; 9 bottom right: GeorgiosArt/iStockphoto; 10: traveler1116/iStockphoto; 11 top: From The New York Public Library; 11 bottom: Library of Congress; 12 background: Roberto A Sanchez/iStockphoto; 12 top: The Granger Collection; 12 bottom left: Everett Collection/age fotostock; 12 bottom right: Everett Collection/age fotostock; 13 top: Library of Congress; 13 bottom: Library of Congress; 14-15 spread: Superstock, Inc.; 15 top: arlindgues/iStockphoto; 15 bottom: The Granger Collection; 16 background: GraphicaArtis/Getty Images; 16 inset: Nikada/iStockphoto; 17 left: Richard Cummins/Superstock, Inc.; 17 right: Richard Cummins/Superstock, Inc.; 17 bottom: icafreitas/iStockphoto; 18 top: Image Asset Management/age fotostock; 18 bottom left: Time Life Pictures/Getty Images; 18 bottom right: SirHenryNorris/Wikimedia; 18 circuitry and throughout: Angus/Fotolia; 19 top: Science and Society/Superstock, Inc.; 19 bottom: Time Life Pictures/Getty Images; 20 left: Mary Evans Picture Library Ltd/age fotostock; 20 right: Photo 12/Getty Images; 21 left: Heritage Images/Getty Images; 21 right: grafvision/iStockphoto; 22 top: Science and Society/Superstock, Inc.; 22 bottom: Science and Society/Superstock, Inc.; 23 top: cosmin4000/iStockphoto; 23 center: halbergman/iStockphoto; 23 bottom: DutchScenery/iStockphoto; 24 top: Chicago History Museum/Getty Images; 24 bottom left: The Granger Collection; 24 bottom right: Library of Congress; 24 flag: 719production/iStockphoto; 25 top: Bettmann/Getty Images; 25 bottom: Hulton Archive/Getty Images; 26, 27: Library of Congress; 28: MarkSwallow/iStockphoto; 29 top: Library of Congress; 29 bottom: Courtesy University of Illinois Press; 29 currency: Terrance Emerson/iStockphoto; 30 top: Bettmann/Getty Images; 30 bottom left, bottom right: Library of Congress; 30 newspaper: paperlessarchives.com/Wikimedia; 31 top: Hulton Archive/Getty Images; 31 bottom: GraphicaArtis/Getty Images; 32: Photo Researchers/Getty Images; 33: Clifford Mueller/iStockphoto; 34: Keen Collection/Getty Images; 35: Amanda Melones/Dreamstime; 36 top: Bettmann/Getty Images; 36 bottom left: Library of Congress; 36 bottom right: Library of Congress; 36 Ouija Board: markham203/Fotolia; 37 top, bottom: Library of Congress; 38 top: ullstein bild/Getty Images; 38 center: duncan1890/iStockphoto; 38 bottom: Library of Congress; 39: Library of Congress; 40 top: Library of Congress; 40 bottom left: muratkoc/iStockphoto; 40 bottom right: bobbidog/iStockphoto; 41 top: ksenon/iStockphoto; 41 bottom left, bottom right: Library of Congress; 42 top: Library of Congress/Superstock, Inc.; 42 bottom left: Madame Marie Curie French Physicist and Chemist (1867-1934)/Superstock, Inc.; 42 bottom right: Nickolas Muray/Herald-Post Collection/Ekstrom Library/ULPA; 42 chalkboard: Hallpoint/Thinkstock; 43 top: The Granger Collection; 43 bottom: Library of Congress; 44 top: Peter van Evert/Alamy Images; 44 bottom: Advertising Archive/Everett Collection; 45 left: Ann Ronan Pictures/age fotostock; 45 right: Zirafek/iStockphoto; 46 top: INTERFOTO/Alamy Images; 46 bottom: cteracterdesign/iStockphoto; 47: Pictorial Press Ltd/Alamy Images; 48 background: John Shearer/Getty Images; 48 main: Everett Collection Inc/Alamy Images; 49 left: Everett Collection; 49 right: Hulton Archive/Getty Images; 50 top left: Everett Collection Inc/Alamy Images; 50 top right: Danny Smythe/Dreamstime; 50 bottom: ullstein bild/Getty Images; 51: New York Daily News Archive/Getty Images; 52: Likelemur/Dreamstime; 53, 54: Bettmann/Getty Images; 55 top: Sueddeutsche Zeitung Photo/The Image Works; 55 bottom: Bettmann/Getty Images; 56 background and throughout: Pingebat/iStockphoto; 56 Tolkien and background: Haywood Magee/Getty Images; 56 Lewis: Hans Wild/Getty Images; 57 left: Keystone Pictures USA/Alamy Images; 57 right: Time Life Pictures/Getty Images; 58 top left: John Chillingworth/Getty Images; 58 top right: Peter Hansen/iStockphoto; 58 bottom: Everett Collection Inc/Alamy Images; 59: Alex Livesey - FIFA/Getty Images; 60: jakubtravelphoto/Shutterstock, Inc.; 61 top: koya79/iStockphoto; 61 bottom: ZargonDesign/iStockphoto; 62 top left: AF archive/Alamy Images; 62 top right and throughout: kreinage/iStockphoto; 62 bottom left: Pictorial Press Ltd/Alamy Images; 62 bottom right: Warner Bros. Pictures/Everett Collection; 63 left: Camera Press/TopFoto/The Image Works; 63 right: Pamela Chandler/ArenaPal/The Image Works; 64 background: dimbreckwoldt/iStockphoto; 64 main: Bettmann/Getty Images; 65 left: Yale Joel/Getty Images; 65 right: Michael Ochs Archives/Getty Images; 66 top left: Umberto Stevenati/AP Images; 66 top right: Nastco/iStockphoto; 66 bottom: Alfred Eisenstaedt/Getty Images; 67: J. R. Eyerman/Getty Images; 68 top: dimbreckwoldt/iStockphoto; 68 center: Library of Congress; 68 bottom: tatniz/iStockphoto; 69: AP Images; 70 left: Evening Standard/Getty Images; 70 right: Gilles Petard/Redferns/Getty Images; 71 top: J. R. Eyerman/Getty Images; 71 bottom: Yale Joel/Getty Images; 72 background: Martin Wahlborg/iStockphoto; 72 main: David Redfern/Getty Images; 73: Rolls Press/Popperfoto/Getty Images; 74 top left and bottom: David Magnus/Shutterstock/Rex USA; 74 top right: DutchScenery/iStockphoto; 75: GAB Archive/Getty Images; 76 top: Superstock, Inc.; 76 bottom: the_guitar_mann/iStockphoto; 77 top: Victor Hugo King/Library of Congress; 77 bottom: FotografiaBasica/iStockphoto; 78: Robert Whitaker/Getty Images; 79: Michael Ochs Archives/Getty Images; 80 background: aptlee/iStockphoto; 80 main: Rob Taggart/Getty Images; 81: Manny Millan/Getty Images; 82 top left and bottom: Larry Marano/Getty Images; 82 top right: by_nicholas/iStockphoto; 83: Jacqueline Duvoisin/Getty Images; 84 top: ImageDB/iStockphoto; 84 center: ABC Photo Archives/Getty Images; 84 bottom: HodagMedia/iStockphoto; 85: Popperfoto/Getty Images; 86: Peter Cosgrove/AP Images; 87: Jean-Yves Ruszniewski/Getty Images; 88 background: Stefano Tiraboschi/iStockphoto; 88 main: Julie Jacobson/AP Images; 89 left: EdStock/iStockphoto; 89 right: Stukley/Dreamstime; 90 top left: Ronald Callaghan/Dreamstime; 90 top right: zlisjak/iStockphoto; 90 bottom: Richard Kane/Dreamstime; 91: Mark J. Terrill/AP Images; 92: Gene J. Puskar/AP Images; 93 top: John Lindsay/AP Images; 93 bottom left: PhotoMelon/iStockphoto; 93 bottom right: wojciechj/iStockphoto; 94 top: shironosov/iStockphoto; 94 bottom: Chris McGrath/Getty Images; 95 top: mbbirdy/Thinkstock; 95 bottom: Chuck Solomon/Getty Images; 96 background: Yen Teoh/iStockphoto; 96 main: Courtesy Patrick Stewart/ID PR; 97 left: Taylor Hill/Getty Images; 97 right: Juliana Parker/Getty Images; 98 top left and bottom: Bruce Glikas/Getty Images; 98 top right: Vasiliki Varvaki/iStockphoto; 99: Courtesy Patrick Stewart/ID PR; 100: Kerry Hayes/Twentieth Century Fox Film Corp./Photofest; 101 top: Photofest; 101 bottom, 102: Courtesy Patrick Stewart/ID PR; 103 top: Dave M. Benett/Getty Images; 103 center: Paramount Television/Photofest; 103 bottom: CTRPhotos/iStockphoto; 104 background and throughout: kosmekodesign/iStockphoto; 104 main: Jeff Kravitz/Getty Images; 105 left: Steve Granitz/Getty Images; 105 right: Starstock/Dreamstime; 106 left: Starstock/Dreamstime; 106 right: VvoeVale/iStockphoto; 107: Kevin Mazur/AMA2014/Getty Images; 108: JXA/Cousart/JFXimages/WENN; 109 top: Library of Congress; 109 center: Star Max/IPx/AP Images; 109 bottom: lucido/iStockphoto; 110-111 spread: Subciaphotography/Dreamstime; 110 inset: enka74/Shutterstock, Inc.; 111 inset: Larry Busacca/LP5/Getty Images; 112 top: Raymond Hall/Getty Images; 112 bottom: Catherine Lane/iStockphoto; back cover: Courtesy Patrick Stewart/ID PR.

Library of Congress Cataloging-in-Publication Data available

ISBN 978-0-545-94253-9

10 9 8 7 6 5 4 3 2 1 17 18 19 20 21

Printed in the U.S.A. 40

First printing, 2017

Book design by Kay Petronio

CONTENTS

Thomas Jefferson
John Adams
Benjamin Franklin

« CHAPTER ONE »

John ADAMS

&

Thomas JEFFERSON

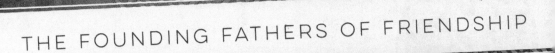

THE FOUNDING FATHERS OF FRIENDSHIP

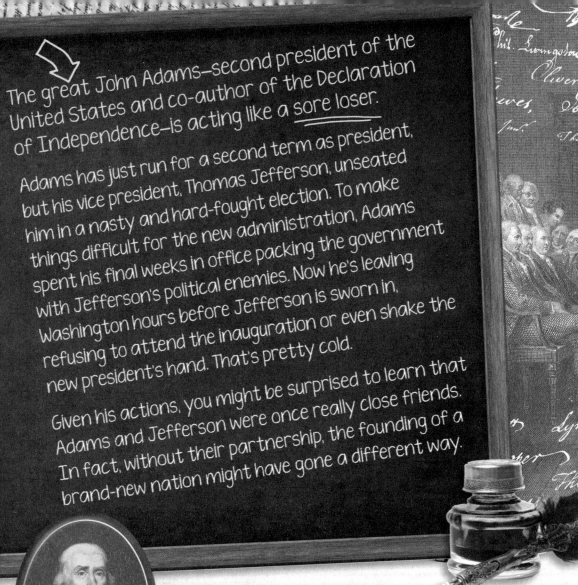

The great John Adams—second president of the United States and co-author of the Declaration of Independence—is acting like a <u>sore loser</u>.

Adams has just run for a second term as president, but his vice president, Thomas Jefferson, unseated him in a nasty and hard-fought election. To make things difficult for the new administration, Adams spent his final weeks in office packing the government with Jefferson's political enemies. Now he's leaving Washington hours before Jefferson is sworn in, refusing to attend the inauguration or even shake the new president's hand. That's pretty cold.

Given his actions, you might be surprised to learn that Adams and Jefferson were once really close friends. In fact, without their partnership, the founding of a brand-new nation might have gone a different way.

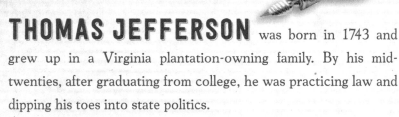

THOMAS JEFFERSON was born in 1743 and grew up in a Virginia plantation-owning family. By his mid-twenties, after graduating from college, he was practicing law and dipping his toes into state politics.

JOHN ADAMS, born in 1735 and raised in Quincy, Massachusetts, graduated from Harvard not quite knowing what he wanted to do with his life. He wondered in his diaries what it meant to have "Honour [sic] or Reputation" and to be "a great Man," eventually landing in a legal career and marriage to his third cousin Abigail Smith (by the way, this used to be considered okay, and not gross). By 1765, Adams was an outspoken critic of British

SIGNING OF THE DECLARATION OF INDEPENDENCE, JULY 4, 1776

rule in America, writing speeches and newspaper articles about unpopular policies like "taxation without representation," which forced Americans to pay heavy taxes to England without giving them any voice in the government.

Jefferson and Adams first met each other in Philadelphia as members of the Continental Congress of 1775. The two men were total opposites: Jefferson was a tall, elegant, and cool-tempered Southern gentleman, while Adams was a short, stout New Englander who loved to argue . . . loudly. Yet they both believed in American independence from Britain and supported a revolution. Jefferson became very close to Adams and Abigail, whom he found charming and intelligent. When it came to Adams, Jefferson clearly saw the man's faults but liked and respected him anyway. In a letter to a friend years later, Jefferson described Adams as "vain" and "irritable," but then went on to write, "He is so amiable that I pronounce that you will love him." Adams made it clear that he admired (and maybe even envied) Jefferson, telling him early

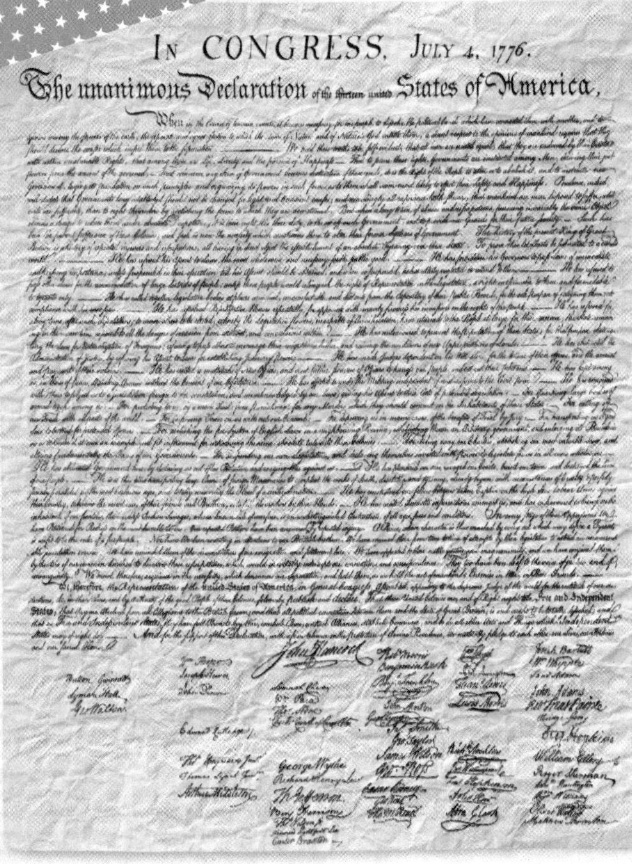

In Congress, July 4, 1776.

The unanimous Declaration of the thirteen united States of America,

in their friendship: "I am obnoxious, suspected and unpopular. You are very much otherwise." If these two men were alive today, they would probably be called "frenemies."

In the summer of 1776, Jefferson and Adams served on the five-man committee that drafted the Declaration of Independence, which officially announced America's split from England. When it came time to put quill to parchment, each believed the other man should write it. Adams won, and the job went to Jefferson, although he didn't present it to Congress until Adams and Benjamin Franklin had a chance to make corrections. Congress still had to ratify and sign the document, and there were members who strongly opposed it. It was up to John Adams to make a final impassioned speech that convinced Congress to sign the Declaration. Adams's skill as a speaker combined with Jefferson's talent for writing changed history and gave birth to a new nation, earning them a place in the group of Americans called the "Founding Fathers."

Party On!

The rivalry between John Adams and Thomas Jefferson led to the two-party system that dominates American politics today. During Washington's presidency, there was only one party: the Federalists. As Jefferson drifted away from the policies of Adams and other Federalists, he and his supporters formed the "Democratic-Republican Party" to separate themselves and their different viewpoints.

After the colonies won the Revolutionary War and the United States became an independent country, the two friends served their new nation as diplomats. Jefferson headed to Paris, while Adams settled in London. They kept up their eighteenth-century "bromance" through letters and visits, touring English gardens and the home of William Shakespeare together. Adams described exchanging letters with Jefferson as "one of the most agreeable events in my life."

George Washington

During the eight years of George Washington's presidency, Jefferson and Adams saw their ideas about government head in different directions, and they ended up running against each other in the election of 1796. Adams won the presidency and Jefferson, finishing second, became vice

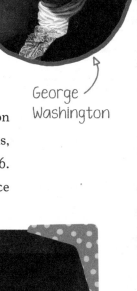

ADAMS AND JEFFERSON: "FRENEMIES"

president (back then, the veep job went to the candidate who placed second, not the president's "running mate"). Their mutual respect and admiration had once been strong enough to survive disagreements, but now they were becoming true rivals. Adams and Abigail felt that Jefferson had betrayed their friendship for politics, and Jefferson believed that Adams was taking the country in the wrong direction.

When Jefferson challenged Adams for the presidency again in 1800, the scene was set for some major drama.

Adams and his Federalist Party believed in building a strong central government with close ties to Great Britain. Jefferson's Republicans wanted a system with more freedom for the individual states and closer ties to France. The United States was still a very new country, and both sides were convinced that a victory by their opponent would mean disaster.

As the election heated up, things got truly awful. The Republicans called Adams "hideous" and a "fool," and made jokes about how he wasn't masculine enough to be president. They said that Adams was a tyrant who would drag America back to monarchy and start a war with France. Meanwhile, Adams's Federalist supporters labeled Jefferson a soft weakling who didn't believe in God. The allegations, half-truths, and shameless lies flew back and forth like poison arrows. Some believed it would lead to civil war and maybe even the end of American democracy. Eventually, the contest was decided by the House of Representatives, which voted more than thirty times before finally giving the presidency to Jefferson.

After the bruising and bashing of that election—many historians consider it to be the fiercest US race ever—the friendship between Adams and Jefferson appeared to be over for good. They eventually retired to their homes in Massachusetts and Virginia, respectively, no longer even corresponding through letters. In 1811, a Virginian visiting Massachusetts heard John Adams say, "I always loved Jefferson, and I still love him." When Jefferson heard this, he wrote to a mutual friend, Dr. Benjamin Rush, who helped the two men reunite. They

THE FIVE-MAN COMMITTEE DRAFTING THE DECLARATION OF INDEPENDENCE

Librarian-in-Chief

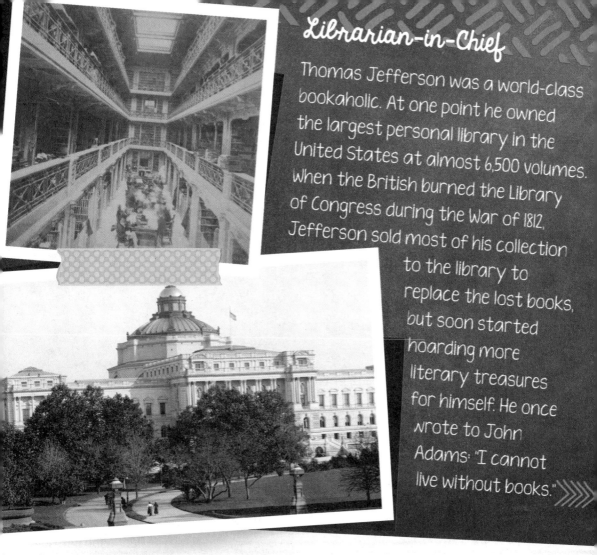

Thomas Jefferson was a world-class bookaholic. At one point he owned the largest personal library in the United States at almost 6,500 volumes. When the British burned the Library of Congress during the War of 1812, Jefferson sold most of his collection to the library to replace the lost books, but soon started hoarding more literary treasures for himself. He once wrote to John Adams: "I cannot live without books."

started writing to each other about all sorts of topics like philosophy, religion, and, of course, politics. The former presidents sent letters back and forth for fifteen years, until they both died.

On the exact same day.

Adams's final thoughts were of his old friend and rival: "Thomas Jefferson survives," he said on his deathbed. He had no way of knowing it, but Jefferson had taken his last breath just hours earlier.

The even weirder part is that the date was July 4, 1826—Independence Day, and the fiftieth anniversary of the vote to approve that great document they'd written together.

Some see this as one of the spookiest coincidences in history, while others say it's destiny. All we know for sure is that two of America's greatest political thinkers, who did so much both as friends and rivals to shape our country in its first fifty years, went out together . . . linked in death just as they were in life.

« CHAPTER TWO »

Meriwether LEWIS & William CLARK

ONE DARING DUO

On January 10, 1809, a husband and wife named William and Julia welcomed their firstborn son to the world. They already had a name picked out. No traditional John or James or Thomas for this kid; their baby was going to be called Meriwether Lewis Clark.

If he got teased for his unique name, maybe he would feel better knowing it was given to him in honor of a famously cool guy: an army captain, a fearless explorer, and his father's partner in America's greatest adventure story.

LEWIS and **CLARK**. You've probably heard the names and noticed how they seem to run together, like "mac and cheese" or "rock 'n' roll." But the reason why these names are forever linked goes much deeper than basic historical facts.

The year was 1801. The newly elected US president, Thomas Jefferson, had hired a man named Meriwether Lewis as his personal secretary and aide, grooming the young army captain for a very special purpose. Jefferson was planning a daring and ambitious mission to explore "the West," which at that time meant pretty much everything west of the Mississippi River. Two years later, Congress voted to fund the expedition, with Lewis as its commander.

Meriwether Lewis was the right man for the job. He was an experienced soldier and proven leader. He was also an outdoorsman and trained naturalist who could study and record the plants and animals of the West. But Lewis was smart enough to know his own limitations, and he knew he couldn't lead an undertaking of this size by himself. He needed a partner who had the skills he didn't. This person had to be someone tough and intelligent whom Lewis could trust completely.

LEWIS AND CLARK EXPEDITION
BY OSCAR EDWARD BERNINGHAUS, 1903-1906

There was one person who fit the bill: William Clark. In 1795, Lewis had been a young officer under Clark's command in a militia unit called "The Chosen Rifle Company." The two men became close friends and respected each other. Now, nearly a decade later, Lewis reached out to his old buddy, writing of their "long and uninterrupted friendship and confidence," and offering him a place in the expedition. Clark happily accepted, writing to Lewis: "My friend, I do assure you that no man lives with whom I would prefer to undertake such a trip as yourself."

Their group of more than two dozen specially trained volunteers was to be known as the "Corps of Discovery." Even though Lewis was the official commander, he saw William Clark as his equal, a co-leader who shared the responsibilities and power to make decisions. He wrote to Clark: "your situation . . . in this mission will in all respects be precisely such as my own." Clark's official rank was second lieutenant, which was lower than Lewis's rank of captain. But Lewis always addressed Clark as Captain, and the other men in the expedition never had a clue that this wasn't Clark's actual rank.

In the military, successful "divided command" is incredibly rare, but somehow Lewis and Clark made it work. Whenever they faced a difficult choice, they usually reached the same decision. When they did disagree, they did it respectfully. They traveled over eight thousand miles together, and there's not a single record of a serious fight or argument between them.

Spelling Struggles

William Clark was great at a lot of things, but he was awful at spelling. Even though many English words didn't have standardized spellings when Clark was learning to write, he took the idea of "creative" spelling to a whole new level in his journals. For example, Clark wrote the word "mosquito" over a dozen different ways, from "muskeetor" to "missquetor." He also managed to find more than twenty ways to spell the Native American tribe "Sioux" even though the word has just five letters!

A PAGE FROM CLARK'S JOURNAL

It may have been their differences, rather than their similarities, that made them such an incredible team. The two men were opposites in many ways. Clark was friendly, outgoing, and even-tempered. Lewis was introverted and prone to dark moods and depression. Although both men were educated, Clark was more practical and rugged, while Lewis tended to be intellectual and philosophical. Clark was a skilled boatman, while Lewis had less experience on the water. They were like two puzzle pieces that fit together. If Lewis lacked some ability, Clark probably had it, and where Clark was weak, Lewis was strong.

Lewis and Clark's epic two-and-a-half-year journey led them up the Missouri River, over the Continental Divide, and down to the Oregon coast and the Pacific Ocean. Together with the men of the Corps and the resourceful Native American woman Sacagawea, they endured freezing temperatures, lack of food, terrifying rapids, dangerous animals, and mountain ranges that were taller, wider, and harder to cross than anything they'd ever seen. Through it all, Clark drew impressively accurate maps. Lewis recorded and collected specimens of plants and animals to bring back to Washington. Both men kept detailed journals that tell us nearly everything they saw, said, and did.

No Coupon Necessary

The Louisiana Purchase was truly the sale of the century. At first, America only wanted to buy the valuable port of New Orleans from France, but when Napoleon offered all 828,000 square miles of Louisiana for just $5 million more (he needed the cash to fund his European invasion habit), Jefferson jumped at the chance. For about three cents an acre, this new territory doubled the size of the United States. Today, fifteen US states are made up, in whole or in part, of that bargain-priced land.

REFINED LEWIS AND RUGGED CLARK

The Lewis and Clark expedition failed in one of its most important goals, which was to find an easy water route to the Pacific. But in every other way, the trip was a stunning success. When historians look at it in terms of its challenges and achievements, it's in the same league as the first American missions to the moon.

Lewis and Clark returned to Washington as heroes and the closest of friends. After an experience like the one they had, it's easy to see how their bond would be cemented . . . a bond proven by Clark's name choice for his new son.

William Clark lived a long and successful life, serving as governor of the Missouri Territory and superintendent of Indian Affairs, and died in 1838. Unfortunately, Lewis could not overcome his lifelong battle with depression: He is believed to have committed suicide in October 1809. Hearing the news, Clark wrote to his brother: "His death is a terrible stroke to me, in every respect."

These two great men had a once-in-a-lifetime kind of friendship, and its legacy will last forever in the maps, history, and culture of the United States.

« CHAPTER 3 »

Charles BABBAGE & Ada LOVELACE

FRIENDSHIP BY THE NUMBERS

England, June 1833. Seventeen-year-old Ada Byron is not your typical Victorian young lady: She's obsessed with math, science, and machines. Fortunately, her private tutor is all for it and introduces her to the famous inventor and mathematician Charles Babbage.

Babbage is impressed with Byron's intelligence and curiosity, and invites her to see something he's built: a small working section of a machine called the "Difference Engine." When completed, the Difference Engine will be a giant mechanical gizmo with metal gears, wheels, and rods, powered by cranking a handle. If it works, it will be used to automatically add up math tables.

In other words, it's the world's first computer, and Ada thinks it's incredibly cool.

And suddenly her own wheels start turning . . .

The friendship between **ADA BYRON** and **CHARLES BABBAGE** was definitely unconventional . . . but then again, so were they.

Ada Byron was born in 1815 to a famous father: the poet Lord George Gordon Byron (Lord Byron for short). Her parents' marriage wasn't a happy one, and Lord Byron left the family when Ada was still a newborn. The divorce made Ada's mother dislike anything having to do with poetry or imagination, so she raised her daughter on a strict diet of science and mathematics. Luckily, Ada was a natural. She was also fascinated by new inventions and even made some of her own, designing boats and steam-powered flying objects.

Her studies were probably a good distraction from her health problems: Ada had chronic headaches that affected her vision,

CALCULATING COMPANIONS: BABBAGE AND BYRON

and when she was thirteen, a case of the measles left her temporarily paralyzed and confined to bed for a whole year. She was determined to walk again, and through sheer determination, she did.

Charles Babbage was born in 1791 and studied mathematics at Trinity College, Cambridge. Better at math than his own teachers, he helped start a group to promote mathematics and find better ways to teach it. After college, he became fascinated by the idea of machines that could do calculations. The British government was interested in this, too, and gave Babbage a grant, or funds, to develop his Difference Engine project.

By the early 1830s, Babbage had experienced a jaw-dropping amount of personal tragedy. In a single year, he lost his father, his son Charles, his newborn son, Alexander, and his beloved wife, Georgiana. He threw himself into his work and London's social scene. Everyone wanted to attend his parties, where an exciting mix of people would gather weekly to discuss the latest in science, literature, art, and other topics.

When they met at a high-society gathering, the young Byron, a debutante, wowed Babbage with her enthusiasm and math smarts. A friend remembered the girl's reaction after Babbage showed her the Difference Engine section; she wrote, "Miss Byron, young as she was, understood its working, and saw the great beauty of the invention." Babbage was much older than Byron, but their minds just clicked. This may have been a huge relief to Byron, who had trouble finding people who took her interests seriously. She visited Babbage several times in the months that followed, and asked him to send her blueprints for the Difference Engine so she could figure out how it worked. Just like that, a friendship was born.

Two years later, at age nineteen, Byron married an aristocrat named William King. Around the same time, she and Babbage began writing to each other. In their letters, they discussed mathematics, logic, science, and technology. Babbage once described Byron as "that Enchantress who has thrown her magical spell around the most abstract of Sciences and has grasped it with a force which few masculine intellects could have exerted over it."

Byron gave birth to three children over the next four years, and when her husband was made Earl of Lovelace, she became Lady Lovelace (Ada Lovelace to historians). Through it all, she continued to study mathematics, pushing herself to tackle more advanced levels.

Techno-Warriors

Long after they both died, Babbage and Lovelace helped the Allies win World War II. Lovelace's notes on the Analytical Engine inspired an Englishman named Alan Turing, who built an early computer to help break the Nazi communications code—an amazing story told in the 2014 film *The Imitation Game*. Over in America, Howard Aiken designed the Mark I computer based on Babbage's work, which was used by the US Navy in the war effort.

Alan Turing

Math: Not Just for Men

It was a common belief during Ada Lovelace's time that women simply didn't have the brain power for complicated ideas. Once, when she was sick, one of her tutors blamed it on the mathematics she'd been working on. He wrote, "The very great tension of mind which they [math] require is beyond the strength of a woman's physical power of application." Fortunately, Lovelace knew, as we do today, that was ridiculous.

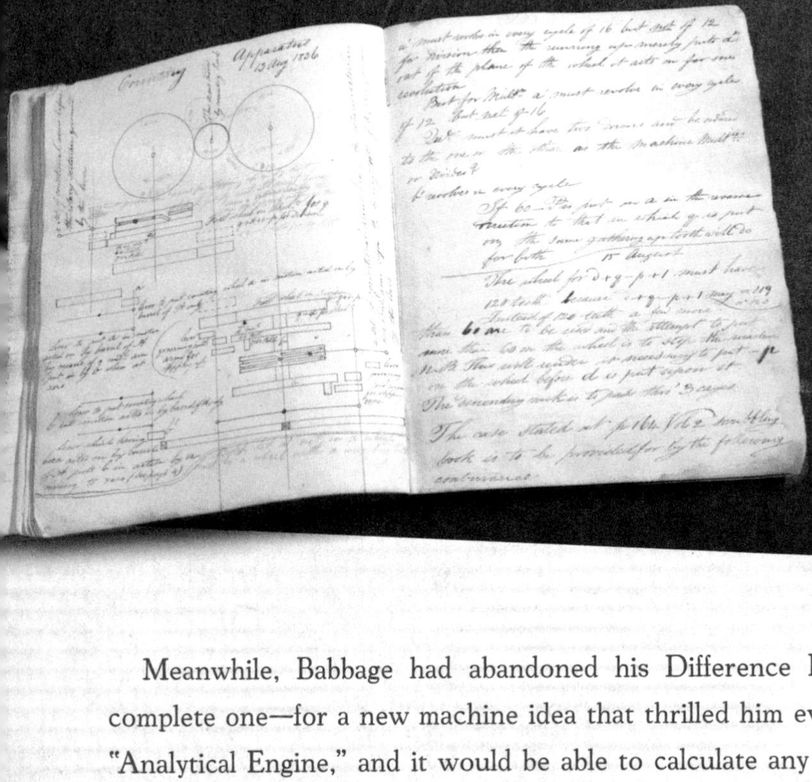

Meanwhile, Babbage had abandoned his Difference Engine—he never built a complete one—for a new machine idea that thrilled him even more. He called it the "Analytical Engine," and it would be able to calculate any mathematical equation or crunch any string of calculations. Babbage even designed a printer to go with it.

During this time, Babbage and Lovelace kept up their friendship. In 1842, when an Italian engineer wrote a short article about the Analytical Engine, Babbage asked Lovelace to translate it for an English publication and even to include her own additions, "as she understood the machine so well." She took that suggestion seriously, adding so many thoughts and ideas that her "notes" ended up being three times longer than the article itself!

In these notes, Lovelace wrote an algorithm—a series of rules to be followed when solving a math problem—that the Engine could use for a set of tricky calculations called "Bernoulli Numbers." She also suggested some outside-the-box notions; for instance, the idea that anything that could be converted into numbers, like music, the alphabet, or symbols, could also be programmed into the machine.

Anything that could be converted into numbers could be programmed into the machine.

Essentially, Lovelace had envisioned a computer that could write music. Today there's an app for that!

She came up with another theory proposing that the Analytical Engine could be told to repeat a series of commands. Turns out, that wasn't just a theory; in today's computer programs, it's called "looping."

Lovelace spent months perfecting the notes, writing back and forth with her friend and mentor, beginning each letter with "My dear Babbage . . ." The paper ended up explaining the Engine and its potential better than even Babbage had been able to, and was published on its own in a science journal. Despite her mother's efforts, Lovelace did have some of her father's poetic imagination, which helped her see a future for the machine beyond what was technologically possible at the time. Because of this, she's often called "the world's first computer programmer."

Shortly after the paper's publication, Lovelace's own potential was cut short when she died of cancer at the age of thirty-six. She chose to be buried next to the father she never knew. Babbage continued his work until his death in 1871 at age seventy-nine, but he never got enough funding to build his Analytical Engine. His inventions, and the ideas they inspired in his friend Ada Lovelace, provided the foundation for the first modern computers built in the 1940s.

These two brilliant minds followed their shared passion to prove that when it comes to friendship—and imagination—anything is possible.

THE COMPTOMETER WAS ONE OF THE FIRST MECHANICAL CALCULATORS.

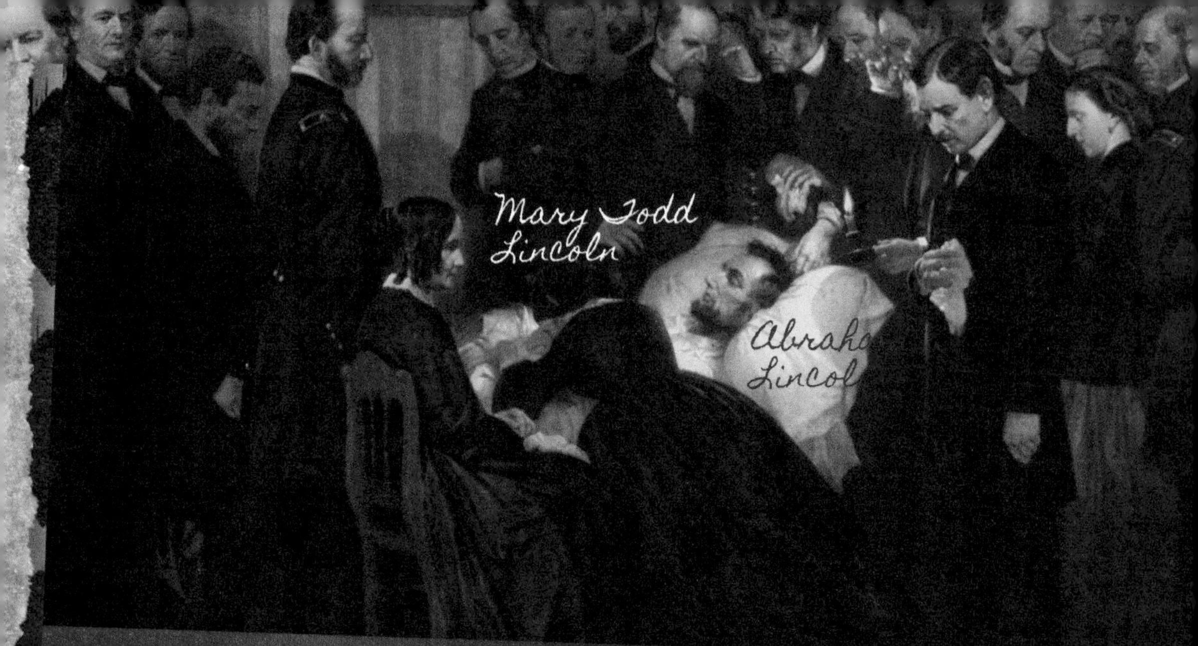

« CHAPTER 4 »

Elizabeth KECKLEY & Mary Todd LINCOLN

BEST FRIEND BETRAYED

April 14, 1865. President Abraham Lincoln's night out at the theater with his wife, First Lady Mary Todd Lincoln, has ended in tragedy. An actor named John Wilkes Booth has shot the president. Lincoln is dying, and Mary is hysterical with shock and grief. Her secretary asks if there's anyone she wants to have with her at this terrible time.

"Yes," says Mary. "Send for Elizabeth Keckley!"

Elizabeth Keckley is a former slave and the First Lady's dressmaker, but Mary isn't calling her for a fashion emergency. Mrs. Lincoln asks for her because now, more than ever, she needs her best friend.

It sounds unlikely: the **FIRST LADY**, who's a Southern belle, besties with a freed slave . . . at the height of the American Civil War? Though the two women's lives began very differently, their paths seemed fated to cross.

ELIZABETH KECKLEY was born sometime in February 1818, on a Virginia plantation owned by Armistead Burwell (he was also her father, but that was a secret she didn't learn until much later). Her mother, Aggy, was a slave, which meant Elizabeth was born a slave, too. From her earliest years, she was put to work sewing, knitting, and watching the Burwell children. When she was four, she accidentally rocked a cradle so hard the baby fell out, and she was brutally whipped as punishment.

Although Elizabeth worked hard, her mistress was cruel and often told her she'd never be "worth [her] salt." At fourteen she was sent to serve the Burwells' oldest son and his demanding wife, and was given the workload of three servants. On several occasions, she was severely beaten without any explanation.

The life of a slave was relentlessly difficult, but there were still some moments of joy. Elizabeth fell in love with a fellow slave named James Keckley and the two got married. Thanks to her mother's sewing lessons, and her own talent and creativity, she also became an amazing seamstress. When money was tight, her master hired her out to make clothing for high-society ladies. Word about Elizabeth's gorgeous outfits soon spread. "With my [sewing] needle," she wrote, "I kept bread in the mouths of seventeen persons for two years and five months."

Unfortunately, James was an alcoholic, and Elizabeth left their unhappy marriage after eight years. She now had only one goal: to buy freedom for herself and her son, George.

In a different state and under very different circumstances, Mary Ann Todd was born in 1818, the same year as Elizabeth. She grew up in a big, wealthy family in Lexington, Kentucky, and a slave she called Mammy Sally raised Mary from birth. After Mary's mother died and her father remarried, she was sent off to boarding school and studied poetry, French, and politics. That was pretty radical for a girl at the time, but Mary wasn't afraid to form and express her own opinions, including her belief that slavery was a hateful, horrible thing that needed to end. She once discovered Mammy Sally giving food to runaway slaves (which was against the law and could have gotten Mammy arrested), but Mary protected her and didn't say a word.

By the time Mary was twenty-one—attractive, witty, charming, and always fashionably dressed—she had plenty of suitors. None of them were interesting enough for her, until she finally met her match in a tall, geeky lawyer named Abraham Lincoln. Her family

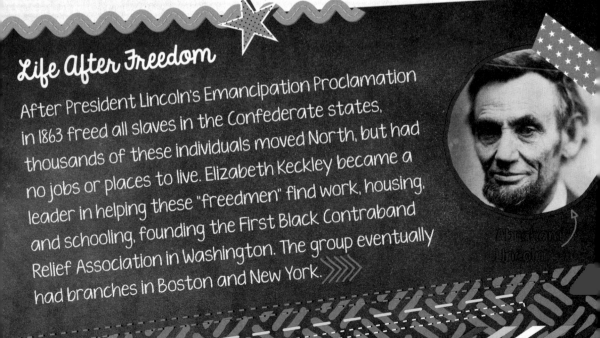

Life After Freedom

After President Lincoln's Emancipation Proclamation in 1863 freed all slaves in the Confederate states, thousands of these individuals moved North, but had no jobs or places to live. Elizabeth Keckley became a leader in helping these "freedmen" find work, housing, and schooling, founding the First Black Contraband Relief Association in Washington. The group eventually had branches in Boston and New York.

Abraham Lincoln

MARY TODD LINCOLN, FIRST LADY

thought he was an uneducated hick, but Mary saw in him a potential for greatness. They were married in 1842. On March 4, 1861, Lincoln was sworn in as the sixteenth president of the United States, proving that Mary was right about his potential.

Even in the 1800s, it was part of the First Lady's job to look elegant and fashionable in public. Mary knew that meant hiring the most talented dressmaker she could find.

Elizabeth Keckley was hoping to get the job. Her hard work, business smarts, honesty, and good nature had endeared her to clients, many of whom helped buy her freedom. Finally, her lifelong dream had come true: She was *free*! To top it off, she was also the most in-demand dressmaker to the A-list ladies of Washington.

There must have been a spark when Elizabeth and Mary met, because Elizabeth got the job and immediately started creating eye-catching and buzzworthy gowns for the First Lady. Mrs. Lincoln liked her dresses fancy, colorful, and low-cut. Before each White House affair, Elizabeth helped dress Mary in one of her designs, arranging her jewelry and hair. Reviewers raved, and Elizabeth's business and social connections grew.

Mary, though, had a tough time making friends in Washington. She had a reputation for being anxious, moody, and hot-headed. With a cabinet full of advisers, Lincoln no longer needed Mary's political opinions. It was lonely at the top for the First Lady . . . and she started confiding in Elizabeth, the one person who was often nearby, ready to help. Maybe the high-strung Mary was comforted by Elizabeth's consistent ability to do a good job, even under pressure. Maybe Elizabeth saw in Mary a person who needed her, and after years of struggling to be recognized as a person, she was proud to be a respected member of the First Lady's entourage. Somehow, these two women from opposite backgrounds created a meaningful friendship.

When Mary's sons Willie and Tad caught typhoid fever, Elizabeth helped Mary nurse the boys day and night. Tad recovered, but eleven-year-old Willie died. Mary was devastated, and Elizabeth took time away from her business to be by Mrs. Lincoln's side. She knew this kind of grief: Her son George had recently been killed on a Civil War battlefield. Elizabeth and Mary were no longer black or white, ex-slave or Southern belle, dressmaker or First Lady. They were mothers in mourning, forever connected.

On April 15, 1865, Elizabeth woke up to the news that Abraham Lincoln was dead. A carriage was waiting to take her to the White House, and she stayed with the First Lady for five weeks. "I was her only companion in the days of her sorrow," she wrote. When Mary finally left Washington for a fresh start in Chicago, she begged Elizabeth to go with her, and at first Elizabeth refused to leave her business. But Mary persisted and eventually Elizabeth agreed.

Not long after, the former First Lady found herself deep in debt and desperate for money. Her attempt to sell her clothes at a public auction was a gigantic failure and the press cruelly called it the "Old Clothes Scandal," labeling Mary "greedy" and a "national disgrace." Eager to help her friend, Elizabeth published a letter in a newspaper defending Mary's actions and asked African American leaders to raise funds for the debt, but with no luck. Elizabeth's reputation was now damaged because she was involved in the scandal. When Mary finally received money from Lincoln's estate, Elizabeth didn't get any of it, even though Mary had promised she would. "If I *ever* get any money you will be remembered, be assured," Mary wrote in a letter to Elizabeth.

Then Elizabeth had an *Aha!* moment. She'd led a pretty interesting life. What if she wrote a book about it? The profits could help Mary pay off her debt. Elizabeth worked with a writer to draft the manuscript, and to prove how close she was with the First Lady, she lent him twenty-three letters Mary had written her on the condition that he wouldn't include anything embarrassing about the Lincoln family. The book was

A First Lady Loses Her Mind

The death of her son Tad in 1871 nearly sent Mary Todd Lincoln over the edge. She began to hear voices, thought the city of Chicago was on fire (it wasn't), and sewed $56,000 of government bonds inside her petticoats. When her son Robert had her committed to an insane asylum, she even attempted suicide.

published with the intriguing title *Behind the Scenes, or, Thirty Years a Slave, and Four Years in the White House.*

The book made a big splash . . . but not in the way Elizabeth was hoping for. Somehow, Mrs. Lincoln's personal letters *did* appear in the book. Mary's son Robert Lincoln was furious that Elizabeth had revealed personal stories about his family. Elizabeth tried to defend herself in the press, reminding them that she was a free woman. Didn't she have a right to tell her story and express her opinions?

But it was too late. Elizabeth's reputation was shattered. She never earned a profit from the book. Worst of all, Mary believed the one person she trusted had betrayed her, and the two women never saw each other again.

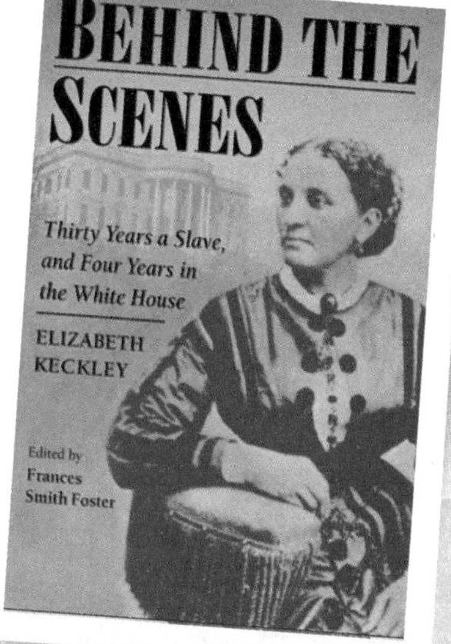

BEHIND THE SCENES
Thirty Years a Slave, and Four Years in the White House
ELIZABETH KECKLEY
Edited by Frances Smith Foster

Mary died in Springfield, Illinois, on July 16, 1882. Elizabeth lived to be eighty-nine, sewing as much as she could in her golden years. In her small bedroom hung a picture of her old best friend, the former First Lady.

Despite the sad ending to their friendship, Elizabeth Keckley and Mary Todd Lincoln were both ahead of their time, letting true connection carry them across barriers of race and status. They were there for each other during some of the most important periods of their lives . . . and in the history of the United States.

PRESIDENT WILSON SAYS:
"This is the time to support Woman Suffrage."

« CHAPTER 5 »

Susan B. ANTHONY & Elizabeth Cady STANTON

PERFECT PARTNERS FOR EQUAL RIGHTS

Revolution.

May 1851, Seneca Falls, New York. Two women are meeting for the first time.

Susan B. Anthony, a former schoolteacher, is in town to attend the same antislavery lecture as Elizabeth Cady Stanton, a busy mother of four kids. They have a mutual friend named Amelia Bloomer, and when the three women randomly find themselves on the same street corner, polite introductions are made.

Stanton wrote later that she liked Anthony's "good earnest face and genial smile" and wanted to have her over for dinner, but she was so busy with her misbehaving children, she completely forgot to ask.

In the end, that single social faux pas didn't matter. There would be plenty of time—fifty-one years to be exact—for Stanton and Anthony to become close friends, work passionately for the causes they cared about, and change the future while they were at it.

Here are just a few things a woman wasn't allowed to do in 1800s America: attend college, own property if she was married, get a divorce, or vote in a political election (also known as "suffrage"). Many people believed that women were less intelligent and generally inferior compared to men.

Enter **ELIZABETH CADY STANTON** and **SUSAN B. ANTHONY**, from two very different directions.

Elizabeth Cady was born in 1815 in Johnstown, New York. She had four sisters, and when the youngest was born, she remembered visitors saying, "What a pity it is she's a girl!" Three of her brothers died as babies, and the only surviving one, Eleazar, died at age twenty. Cady tried to fill the gap in her family

The Women's Wild West

While suffragists were fighting for an amendment to the US Constitution, the battle was also being fought state by state, with many victories. Wyoming was a trailblazer, the first state to give women the vote, followed by Colorado Utah, and Idaho.

by doing things she described as "learned and courageous" that were usually reserved for boys. She jumped obstacles on horseback, challenged male students to debate, and was the only girl at Johnstown Academy to study Greek.

After graduating from high school, Cady was drawn to social reform: the abolition (ending) of slavery, temperance (not drinking alcohol), and women's rights. She fell in love with a forward thinker named Henry Stanton, and when they tied the knot in 1840, they agreed it would be a marriage of equals. In a radical move, they cut the word "obey" from their wedding vows.

Susan B. Anthony was born in 1820 on a Massachusetts farm. Her family belonged to the Religious Society of Friends, known as Quakers, a branch of Christianity that believes in simplicity in daily life and worship, so toys, games, and music were forbidden. Books were their main source of entertainment and Anthony learned to read by age four.

The Quakers also believed every human had a duty to be useful to the world, and that women should be allowed to express themselves. Anthony's father, Daniel, made sure that *all* his children, sons and daughters, got the highest-quality education. By the time she was fifteen, Anthony was working as a teacher.

In 1848, Stanton was raising three boys, running her own household, and totally bored. She went looking for a way to "remedy the wrongs of society and of woman in particular," as she wrote, and helped organize a Woman's Rights Convention in

Seneca Falls, NY. She drafted a statement to outline the group's mission and called it the "Declaration of Sentiments" as a nod to the Declaration of Independence.

Around the same time, Anthony was tired of being a teacher and joined a local society promoting temperance, where her leadership skills earned her the nickname "Napoleon." By 1850, she felt strongly about women's rights and the abolition of slavery, and longed to make a difference. She was great at organizing people and publicity events but not at writing. She once said, "Whenever I take my pen in hand, I always seem to be mounted on stilts."

In contrast, Stanton was a skilled writer. But she could never find the time to get out and share her words since she had a whole bunch of kids at home who needed her. Anthony, meanwhile, was unmarried and could devote time and energy to renting halls for lectures, raising money, gathering petition signatures, and speaking to whatever crowd might listen.

In other words, each had what the other needed.

The two women quickly became close friends. Stanton shared her knowledge of politics, the law, philosophy, and self-expression. Anthony listened and pushed back with questions and critiques. Together, they were ready to make a difference.

In their first team-up, they fought for women in New York to be able to own property, engage in business, manage their own income, and have joint guardianship of their children. Anthony traveled throughout the state, speaking and handing out pamphlets. Stanton was a behind-the-scenes mastermind, doing legal research and writing the speeches and literature. ("I forged the thunderbolts and she fired them," Stanton once said about Anthony.) When Stanton was able to travel and deliver her own speeches, she truly wowed her audiences.

Before and during the Civil War, the duo wrote and spoke against slavery, often facing angry mobs. They helped gather four hundred thousand signatures to persuade Congress to pass the thirteenth Amendment to the Constitution, which ended slavery and gave African Americans their freedom.

After the war, Anthony and Stanton saw an opportunity. The US Constitution was already being expanded to give African Americans additional rights, so couldn't Congress add another amendment to give women the right to vote? Other activists rejected this idea, arguing that African American men should get the vote before women. Anthony and Stanton felt betrayed but didn't give up the cause. Together they formed

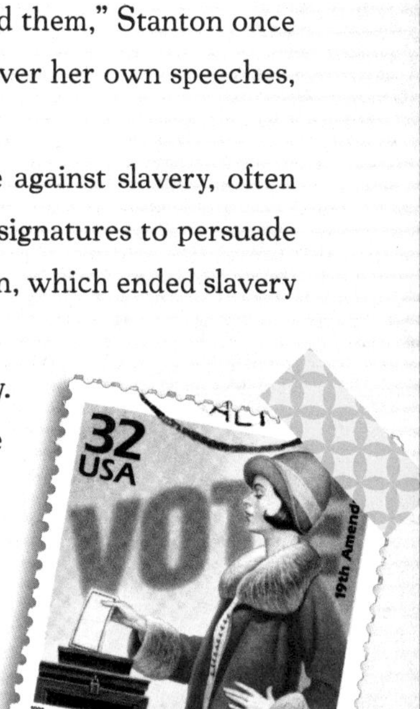

STANTON AND ANTHONY: SERIOUS ABOUT SUFFRAGE

the National Woman Suffrage Association, led by women and focused on getting a constitutional amendment that would guarantee women's right to vote.

Around this time, Stanton wrote, "So closely interwoven have been our lives, our purposes and experiences, that, separated, we have a feeling of incompleteness . . ." She and Anthony worked on many causes together, and eventually their suffrage association joined forces with a rival organization to become the National American Woman Suffrage Association (NAWSA). Stanton was president until 1892, and then Anthony took over until 1900.

In 1895, Stanton published a controversial book called *The Woman's Bible*, in which she rewrote passages from the Bible that she felt were demeaning to women. NAWSA was worried this would hurt their cause and passed a resolution separating the organization from Stanton. Stanton urged Anthony to quit the presidency in protest, but Anthony was torn. Who should she be loyal to: her old friend, or the organization they'd spent so many years building? Anthony decided to stay in office and continue as a mentor to young women who would lead the movement into the future.

They grew apart for a while, but in 1902, Anthony visited Stanton at her new home in New York City. The women had a great time together, hugging and weeping when Anthony left. She promised to return for Stanton's eighty-seventh birthday in November, writing a letter to her friend reminiscing about how it had been "fifty-one years since we first met and we have been busy through every one of them, stirring up the world . . ."

Sadly, they never got the chance to see each other again. When Stanton died of heart failure two weeks before that birthday, Anthony was devastated. "If I had died first," she told a reporter, "she would have found beautiful phrases to describe our friendship, but I cannot put it into words." In keeping with Stanton's wishes, women were completely in charge of her funeral, and a portrait of Anthony was placed on top of the casket, surrounded by flowers.

Anthony forged on without her best friend for almost four more years, supervising NAWSA despite her age and failing health. She never stopped believing that suffrage for women was attainable, insisting that "Failure is Impossible," until she died on March 13, 1906. Fourteen years later, on August 26, 1920, the Nineteenth Amendment to the US Constitution finally passed, giving women the right to vote.

If Stanton and Anthony hadn't found each other when they did, our nation's history might be very different. Undeniably brilliant visionaries and leaders, these two friends had an amazing ability to see the big picture. Their great affection for each other kept them fighting for the changes they cared most about . . . together.

In Mint Condition

Susan B. Anthony was chosen to appear on a new dollar coin in 1979, the first woman to be depicted on American currency. At first, the coin was a big flop because it looked and felt too much like a quarter, and people kept confusing one for the other. But it eventually proved to be useful in vending machines, subways, and buses, and was reissued again in 1999.

« CHAPTER 6 »

Arthur Conan DOYLE & Harry HOUDINI

FRIENDS IN "SPIRIT"

Atlantic City, New Jersey, 1922. The famous magician Harry Houdini is having an awkward moment.

He's on vacation with the writer Arthur Conan Doyle, his good friend, and their wives. Doyle has finally gotten Houdini to participate in a séance to contact Houdini's dead mother, Cecelia. As the two men watch, Doyle's wife, Jean, goes into a deep trance, then begins writing down messages from "Cecilia" to her son.

The only problem? The notes are in perfect English, a language that Cecelia could barely speak while she was alive. Houdini also has a hard time believing his Jewish mother would start off by having Jean draw a Christian cross on the paper.

Houdini knows Jean's "powers" aren't real. He can't decide if he should admit this or lie to spare the feelings of his good friend. Were the Doyles trying to fool Houdini, or were they fooling themselves? If Houdini does speak his mind, will his friendship with Doyle survive?

Both **HARRY HOUDINI** and **ARTHUR CONAN DOYLE** became famous for creating mystery, but they came from very different worlds.

Doyle was brought up as a young gentleman of privilege. Born in 1859 into a Scottish family with wealthy relatives, he attended private schools, and by age twenty-one he was working as a doctor. His real love, though, was writing short stories, and in 1886 he created a fictional detective named Sherlock Holmes. The first Holmes mystery, *A Study in Scarlet*, was an instant hit. In a few short years, the character made Doyle an internationally successful author. He eventually got the urge to branch out and took a long break from the Holmes character starting in 1893. After that, he ran a hospital in South Africa during the Boer

DOYLE, THE MASTER OF MYSTERIES

War, wrote stories about a new character named Dr. Challenger, and served as a correspondent during World War I.

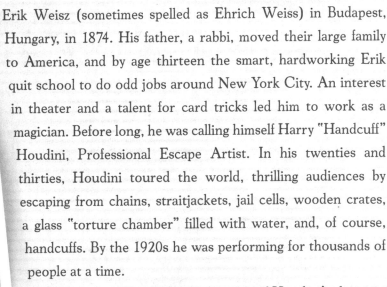

Harry Houdini started out in much more humble circumstances. He was born Erik Weisz (sometimes spelled as Ehrich Weiss) in Budapest, Hungary, in 1874. His father, a rabbi, moved their large family to America, and by age thirteen the smart, hardworking Erik quit school to do odd jobs around New York City. An interest in theater and a talent for card tricks led him to work as a magician. Before long, he was calling himself Harry "Handcuff" Houdini, Professional Escape Artist. In his twenties and thirties, Houdini toured the world, thrilling audiences by escaping from chains, straitjackets, jail cells, wooden crates, a glass "torture chamber" filled with water, and, of course, handcuffs. By the 1920s he was performing for thousands of people at a time.

Houdini and Doyle first met at one of Houdini's shows in England in 1920 and realized they were both fascinated with spiritualism, the growing belief that the dead exist in a spirit world and can communicate with the living. But they didn't feel the same way about it. Houdini was an illusionist with seemingly superhuman abilities, yet when it came to spiritual powers he was a total skeptic. He assumed everything was fake until he could find evidence to prove otherwise. Doyle was famous for creating a character that relied on fact, logic, and rational thinking, but the author firmly believed that most psychics and mediums (people who claimed they could speak to the dead) were the real thing. Even though Houdini and Doyle looked at spiritualism with opposite viewpoints, they liked and respected each other, and became close friends.

Because Houdini was an experienced magician, he knew how easy it was to fool people with fake "supernatural" events. He had spent years in vaudeville theater, where phony psychics made money off gullible, desperate people. Through letters and during visits with Doyle, Houdini tried his best to convince his friend that the spooky "evidence" of the spirit realm was nothing more than cheap parlor tricks and mechanical props. He once demonstrated how ghostly "spirit hands" could be made with simple rubber gloves and wax, but Doyle gave his standard response: Even though Houdini could duplicate something, that didn't mean the original wasn't real. Houdini's campaign to win over Doyle ended up having the reverse effect: The more illusions he performed for the author, the more Doyle became convinced they couldn't just be tricks. He thought they must be evidence that Houdini himself had spiritual powers but just didn't know it! "This ability to unbolt locked doors," Doyle said, "is undoubtedly due to Houdini's mediumistic powers."

It was a viewpoint that must have been incredibly frustrating for Houdini.

Sly Foxes

The modern spiritualist movement began in 1848 in Hydesville, a town near Rochester, New York, when twelve-year-old Kate Fox and her fifteen-year-old sister, Margaret, claimed spirits were "speaking" to them with knocking sounds. With their older sister, Leah, the Fox sisters soon became famous mediums, and by 1850, hundreds of people were attending their séances. In 1888, Kate and Leah admitted they'd faked the whole thing. Despite their confession, the movement they helped launch survives to this day.

Milking the Suspense

One of Houdini's most famous tricks was being handcuffed and sealed into a large metal milk can filled with water and hidden behind a curtain. He'd then emerge several long minutes later, dripping and gasping for air. In reality, the milk can was designed to secretly open at its neck. Houdini would pop out immediately, then relax reading a newspaper backstage until he decided he had tortured his audience long enough.

When the Doyle and Houdini families went on vacation together to Atlantic City in June 1922, Doyle saw an opportunity to change Houdini's mind and arrange a connection with the spirit of the magician's mother. Houdini's heart and mind told him the séance wasn't real, even though he deeply wanted it to be. "I was willing to believe, even wanted to believe," he wrote.

Out of respect for his friends, Houdini kept his thoughts on the ordeal to himself until later that year, when he spoke publicly about how he knew his mother's spirit wasn't really in the room. He didn't think the Doyles were trying to trick him—they were just victims of their own desire to believe, too.

This difference in beliefs was a huge blow to Houdini and Doyle's friendship. Things got worse in the years that followed as Houdini went on a mission to expose fraudulent psychics and mediums, including some whom Doyle had publicly supported. Doyle responded angrily in a 1923 letter: "You cannot . . . attack a subject and yet expect courtesies from those that honor that subject," he wrote to Houdini. "It is not reasonable." In other words, if Houdini kept trying to disprove Doyle's beliefs, they could no longer be friends. Still, Houdini wouldn't budge.

Harry Houdini died in 1926, nine days after he let a young fan hit him four times in the stomach to prove he could survive any punch. Houdini's appendix ruptured, and he refused medical help until it was too late. Doyle followed his former buddy to the grave four years later. The different opinions that drew the two together and energized their connection ultimately doomed their friendship. They never reconciled from that big fight, at least not in this world. But in the world beyond . . . who knows?

Spiritualism: magic or mumbo jumbo?

THE BELIEVER AND THE SKEPTIC

« CHAPTER 7 »

Marie CURIE & Missy MELONEY

THE SHRINKING VIOLET AND THE SOCIAL BUTTERFLY

May 1921. The famous scientist Marie Curie is about to get the thing she wants most in the world.

It weighs about the same as a paper clip, costs $100,000, and can only be presented at the White House by the president of the United States. What is this precious item? A gram of radium, the element Marie helped discover but can't actually afford to buy.

All that's been fixed by the woman who's standing nearby. Her name is Missy Meloney. Only a year ago, she and Marie Curie were strangers . . . but today, Missy is the most important person in Marie's life.

If you've ever had a friend who knows just how to help you when you really need it, **MARIE** and **MISSY'S** story may sound familiar.

Marie Skłodowska was born in Warsaw, Poland, in 1867 and threw herself into science at an early age, eventually moving to Paris to study physics. Sometimes, she'd be so engrossed in her work that she'd forget to eat and would faint from hunger. She met Pierre Curie, who was just as brilliant, passionate, and nerdy as she was, and they married in 1895 (Marie wore a dark blue outfit instead of a wedding gown so she could reuse it as lab wear). Three years later, they announced their discovery of an element they called "polonium" in honor of Marie's home country. Then they discovered radium, named after the Latin word for "ray," and came up with the term "radioactivity." It didn't take long for a profitable industry to form around the production of this glowing stuff. People were excited because it damaged living tissue, which meant it might be used to fight illnesses like cancer.

In 1903, Pierre Curie and another scientist, Henry Becquerel, were awarded the Nobel Prize in Physics. Originally, Marie was shut out because of her gender, but after

Nobel Prize

Pierre complained, her name was added and she became the first woman to win a Nobel. In between all this history-making, the Curies had two daughters, Irène and Ève. But tragedy struck in 1906 when Pierre was fatally hit by a horse-drawn vehicle crossing the street. Marie was devastated but wanted to continue their work. She was given her own radioactivity lab, earned a second Nobel Prize (in Chemistry), and oversaw the installment of X-ray vehicles in field hospitals during World War I. By 1921, Madame Curie was an international celebrity.

Another Marie, nicknamed "Missy," was born in 1878 and grew up in Kentucky. She was a budding concert pianist until a horseback riding accident at age fifteen left her with a damaged leg. Her mother was a journalist and she decided to try that instead, becoming a reporter for the *Washington Post* when she was still a teenager. She summed up her can-do attitude when she said, "I have been lame since fifteen, and had a bad lung since seventeen and have done the work of three men ever since." Missy Meloney was one of the first women to earn a seat in the US Senate's press gallery. She had her own newspaper column at the *New York Sun*, and eventually became the editor of a popular women's magazine called the *Delineator*.

BEFORE *PEOPLE MAGAZINE*, THERE WAS THE *DELINEATOR*.

Missy had interviewed larger-than-life figures such as Benito Mussolini, but what she really wanted was an exclusive with Marie Curie, the person who most inspired her. Problem was, Marie hated the press, and whenever Missy requested an interview, Marie wouldn't respond. Finally, Missy changed her strategy and wrote Marie this note:

My father, who was a medical man, used to say that it was impossible to exaggerate the unimportance of people. But you have been important to me for twenty years, and I want to see you [for] a few minutes.

Something about that note struck a chord with Marie, and she agreed to meet Missy. When they met, Missy saw what she later described as "a pale, timid little woman in a black cotton dress, with the saddest face I had ever looked upon." She wondered why the great Madame Curie had a shabby office and a small apartment, while famous American scientists like Thomas Edison and Alexander Graham Bell were rich. Then Marie dropped a bomb: She had almost no radium to continue her research. She and Pierre had never patented their element, believing their work was for science and not profit, and now it was too expensive for her to buy.

In an instant, Missy's new purpose in life was to help this woman whom she saw as a real hero. She told Marie she was going to get her that radium and whatever else she needed.

Missy went back to America and launched a nationwide campaign to alert people about Marie Curie's dilemma. She played up the drama to tug at people's heartstrings. *With more radium, Marie Curie can find a cure for cancer! Marie Curie has selflessly given so much and now look, she's poor!* It wasn't quite true, but that didn't matter. Women had just won the right to vote a year earlier and were feeling pretty powerful. The campaign was a huge success, and with many people donating small amounts, the $100,000 needed to buy a gram of radium was raised.

Americans had officially caught "Marie-mania." Missy arranged a tour of the United States for Marie and her daughters, which would end with Marie receiving her radium at the White House. Fans waited for five hours to see Marie's ship arrive in New York. Missy coached Marie through her first big interview on the deck of the boat, with dozens of reporters crowding around her.

It Doesn't Grow on Trees

There was a good reason for radium's gigantic price tag: In 1921, it took 500 tons of raw mined rock, 500 tons of chemicals, 1,000 tons of coal, 10,000 tons of water, and labor equal to 350 people working for a full month to produce one single gram of the element, which weighs only about as much as a US dollar bill.

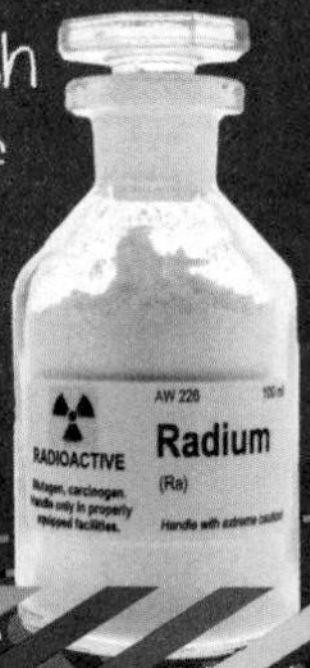

For the next seven weeks, Marie and Missy traveled like celebrities from state to state, receiving awards, visiting laboratories, and spending quality time with Marie's daughters. Marie was exhausted and her health suffered, but by the time she reached that big moment at the White House to receive her radium, the scientist had conquered her fear of the spotlight. With all this money, equipment, and support, she'd be able to continue her research for a long time.

After that trip, Marie was able to talk more openly with her daughters and colleagues about her projects. She got out and socialized more, too. Her world had literally expanded, with many new professional contacts, and that broadened the scope of her work.

Missy and Marie remained close friends for the rest of their lives. Whenever Marie or one of her daughters came to Missy for help, Missy never hesitated to use her influence to make things happen. Perhaps she enjoyed being a part of history instead of just writing about it.

In the end, Marie's years of exposure to radium took their toll. Her eyesight was failing, her fingertips were cracked and scarred, and she was constantly weak and feverish. She eventually developed a form of anemia that led to her death in 1934 at age sixty-six.

Making Mom Proud

Curie's two daughters, Irène and Ève, followed in their mother's high-achieving footsteps. Irène became a scientist and won the Nobel Prize in Chemistry in 1935 for the discovery of artificial radioactivity. Ève built a career as an accomplished writer, journalist, and humanitarian.

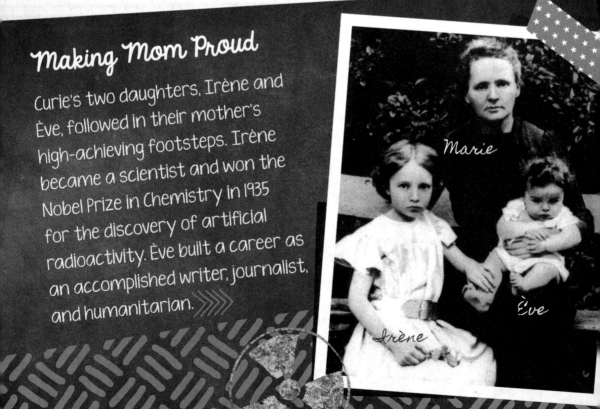

A LIFE DEDICATED TO DISCOVERY

Missy kept working to raise public awareness of issues she cared about, like health, nutrition, and better home construction standards. When she died in 1943 at age sixty-four, another famous friend of hers, Eleanor Roosevelt, honored Missy by writing, "She believed that women had an important part to play in the future."

The radium Marie received that day at the White House may have cost $100,000, but the gifts these two friends brought each other—through kindness, respect, and generosity—were priceless.

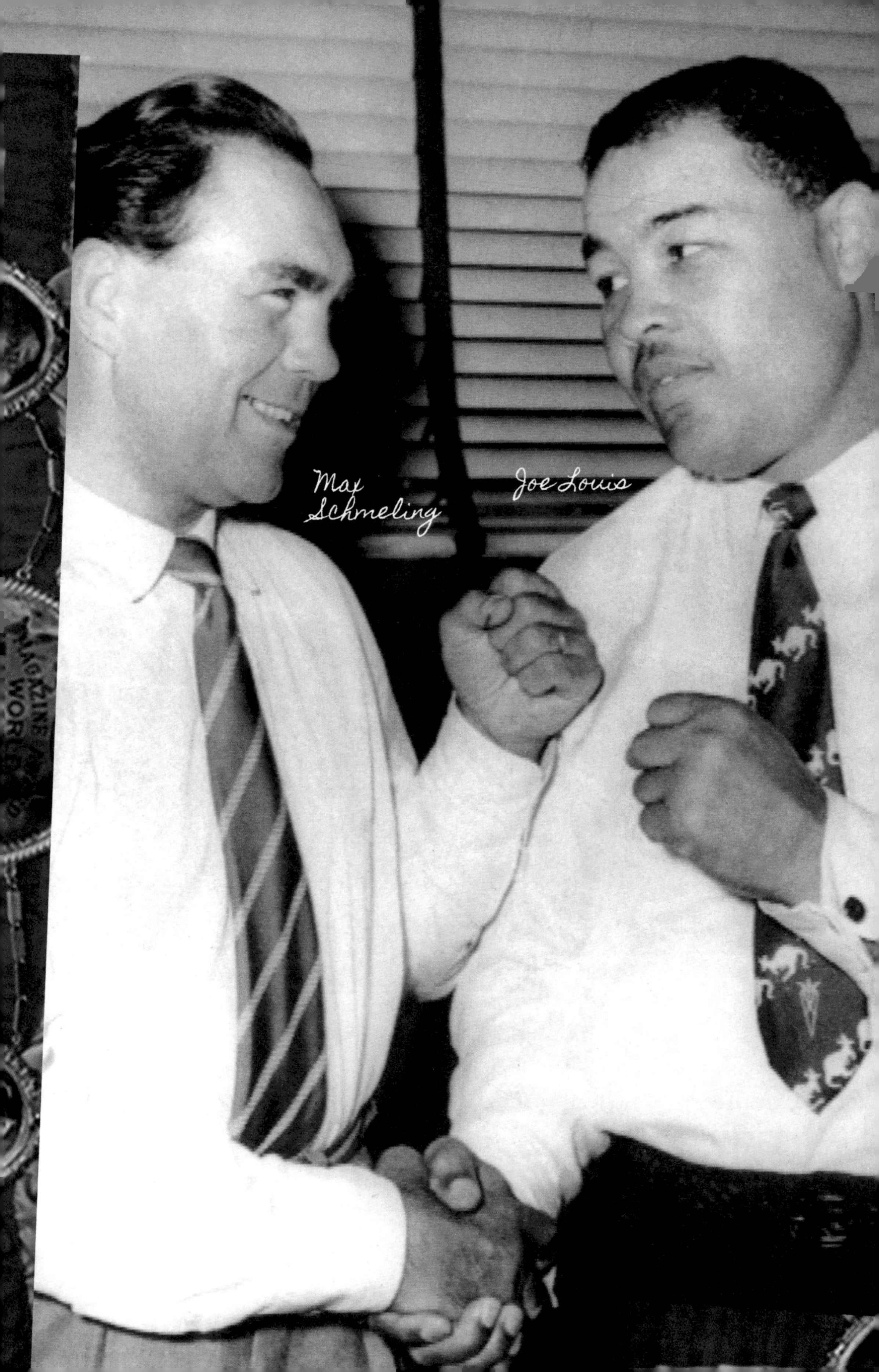
Max Schmeling
Joe Louis

« CHAPTER 8 »

Joe LOUIS

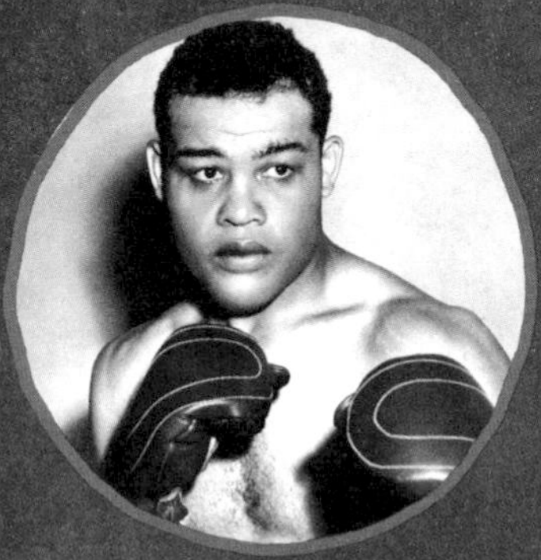

&

Max SCHMELING

WHAT ARE WE FIGHTING FOR?

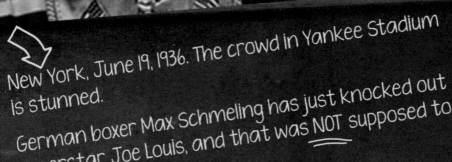

New York, June 19, 1936. The crowd in Yankee Stadium is stunned.

German boxer Max Schmeling has just knocked out superstar Joe Louis, and that was NOT supposed to happen.

Louis, an African American boxer nicknamed the "Brown Bomber," has never been beaten in his professional career. All across the United States, people who turn to sports as an escape from the troubles of the Great Depression are devastated by this loss. In Schmeling's home country, though, folks are celebrating. Adolf Hitler and his Nazi party have taken control of Germany, and many see Schmeling's victory as proof of the Nazi belief that white "Aryans" are superior to other races.

Louis and Schmeling were just doing their job, but somehow they've found themselves fighting on the world stage.

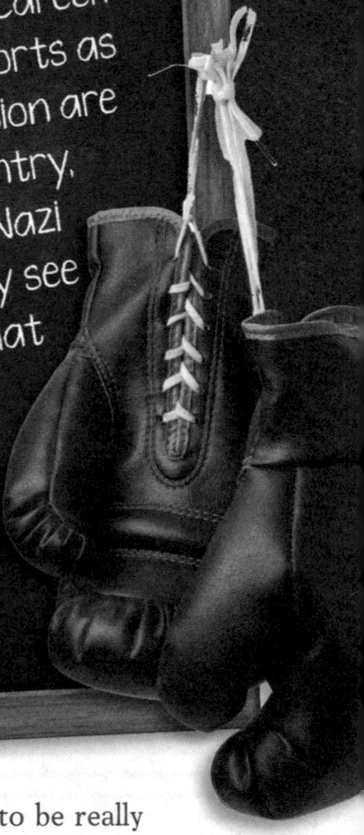

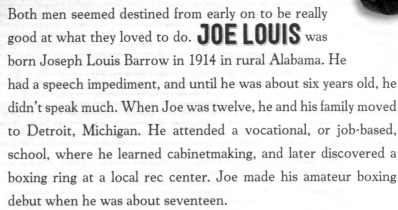

Both men seemed destined from early on to be really good at what they loved to do. **JOE LOUIS** was born Joseph Louis Barrow in 1914 in rural Alabama. He had a speech impediment, and until he was about six years old, he didn't speak much. When Joe was twelve, he and his family moved to Detroit, Michigan. He attended a vocational, or job-based, school, where he learned cabinetmaking, and later discovered a boxing ring at a local rec center. Joe made his amateur boxing debut when he was about seventeen.

MAX SCHMELING was born in Germany in 1905. Boxing was not very popular there, but Schmeling's father was a ship's navigator and had seen the sport during his travels. When he took his teenage son to see one of American boxer Jack

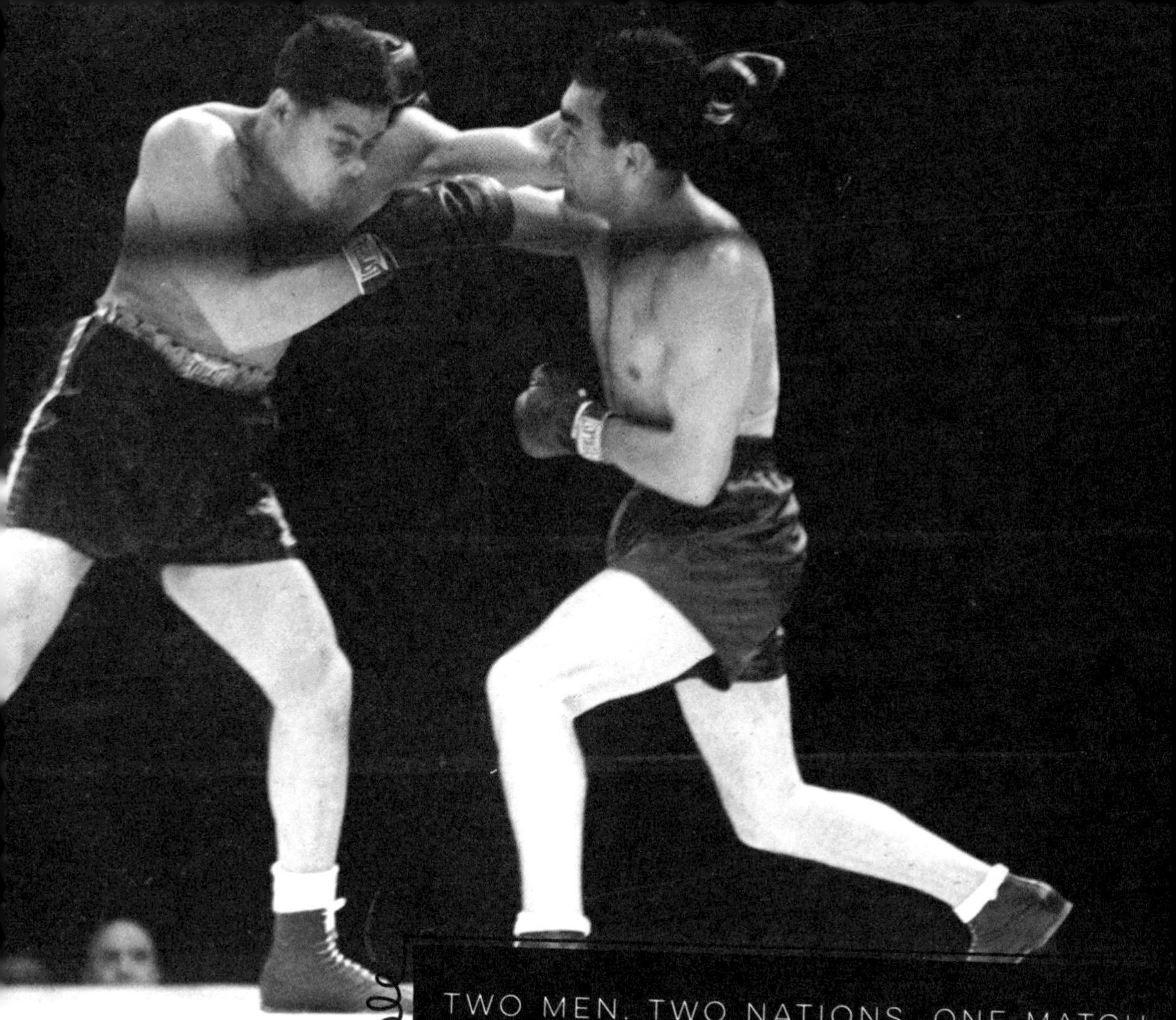
TWO MEN. TWO NATIONS. ONE MATCH.

Dempsey's matches on film, Max was instantly hooked. Dempsey became Schmeling's hero, and Schmeling left home to find a place where he could train to fight just like him.

Schmeling was the heavyweight champion of the world from 1930 to 1932. But by 1936, at the ripe old age of thirty, he was considered past his prime, while young Louis was a star on the rise. When the two were finally scheduled to meet in the ring, sports writers and boxing experts echoed the opinion of most American fans: Louis's victory was a sure thing, and Schmeling was doomed.

In the weeks before the big match-up, Louis spent a lot of time playing golf, while Schmeling was training hard. Analyzing Louis's fighting style, Schmeling found a weakness: Louis had a bad habit of dropping his left hand. On the night of the fight, Schmeling took advantage of this, hitting Louis with his right over and over again. Louis couldn't find a way to stop him, and Schmeling finally delivered a knockout punch to his opponent's jaw in the twelfth round.

It was the punch felt around the world. African Americans in particular saw Louis as a hero and took the loss hard. Writer Langston Hughes wrote: "All across the country that night when the news came that Joe was knocked out, people cried." Meanwhile, Adolf Hitler sent congratulations to Schmeling's wife, and Schmeling told a reporter that he had won the match for his homeland.

The fight sparked feelings of patriotism and pride, but it was nothing compared to the rematch . . .

A year later, Joe Louis did manage to become the heavyweight champion of the world. The title felt empty, though, if he couldn't beat Schmeling, so he trained hard and looked forward to the chance to redeem himself. "I knew I had to get Schmeling good," he later wrote. "The whole country was depending on me."

Louis wasn't exaggerating. In the two years following the first fight, relations between Germany and the United States had completely broken down. The German army had taken over neighboring Austria, and the Nazis were brutally persecuting Jews and other minorities. The world was on the brink of all-out war. When the Louis-Schmeling rematch was announced, people saw it as the Stars and Stripes versus the swastika, the symbol of the Nazis.

Playing Not-So-Nice

Sports and politics often take center stage at the Olympic Games. In 1936, the Nazis used the Berlin Olympics to promote the idea of German superiority. In 1980, the United States boycotted the Moscow Olympics to protest the Soviet invasion of Afghanistan, and four years later the Soviets got payback by refusing to send their athletes to the games in Los Angeles. Because of their racist policy of apartheid, South Africa was banned from the Olympics for nearly three decades, missing all Olympics held from 1964 to 1992.

THE FIGHTER MEETS THE FÜHRER.

Hitler portrayed Schmeling as an example of German power and said that Louis could never defeat their white champion. Germans bragged that Schmeling's prize money would buy more tanks to crush Germany's enemies. For many Americans, Schmeling went from just another opponent to a Nazi villain who embodied everything they hated or feared about Hitler's Germany.

In reality, this version of Schmeling was completely manufactured by Hitler's followers. The German boxer never said he had to "uphold the honor of the white race," or that black men were "inferior." Nazis wrote these words for him. Schmeling's manager, Joe Jacobs, was Jewish, and the champ refused to fire him. He also chose not to join the Nazi Party, and when Hitler tried to give him a medal, Schmeling turned it down—a dangerous move. Schmeling said he was "a fighter, not a politician."

Louis felt his share of pressure, too. US President Franklin Roosevelt met with him and said, "Joe, we need muscles like yours to beat Germany." By the time the two boxers stepped into the ring on June 28, 1938, they were more than just athletes; they were representatives of their nations.

After the monumental buildup, the actual fight turned out to be a one-sided slaughter. From the first bell, Louis mercilessly pummeled Schmeling, knocking him to the canvas three times in less than two minutes. The match lasted just one hundred twenty-four seconds, and Louis finally got his win. Celebrations erupted on the streets of New York.

When the United States officially entered World War II against Germany and the Axis powers on December 11, 1941, Louis served the army by entertaining the troops. When the war ended, he resumed his boxing career and went on to defend his title a record twenty-five times in a row. Louis remained the heavyweight champion until 1949 and is considered one of the greatest boxers of all time.

The Nazis sent Schmeling into combat, perhaps as punishment for his loss in the ring. He was wounded in battle but survived, and later became a successful investor

CHAMPIONS COMPETE AGAIN . . .
BUT THIS TIME JUST FOR LAUGHS.

Schmeling's List

On November 9, 1938, the Nazis began arresting Berlin's Jewish citizens in a night of violent attacks known as *Kristallnacht.* Two young Jewish brothers named Henri and Werner Lewin managed to escape the terror, thanks to Max Schmeling. He hid the teenagers in his suite at a Berlin hotel, telling the staff he was sick and shouldn't be disturbed. Later, he helped the boys leave the country, saving them from near-certain death in a concentration camp. Schmeling never sought publicity for this act of bravery, and the story remained unknown until Henri Lewin revealed the truth at a 1989 banquet honoring the famous boxer.

and wealthy businessman in postwar Germany. In 1954, Schmeling visited the United States and decided to drive to Louis's home in Chicago. He wanted to tell his former rival that he had no bad feelings toward him. The two men talked about the old days and found that they actually got along really well. From there, a friendship emerged between the former rivals.

When Louis had money troubles in the 1950s, Schmeling quietly loaned him money. When Louis got a job greeting guests at a big casino, Schmeling flew to Las Vegas every year to visit him. And when Louis died in 1981, Schmeling served as a pallbearer at his funeral. By this time, the two men, whom the world had once cast as bitter enemies, had been close friends for nearly three decades.

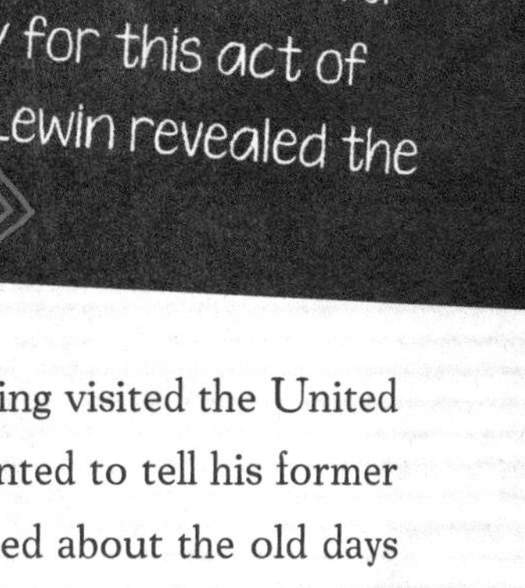

Friends 'til the end.

Schmeling lived a long life and died in 2005 at the age of ninety-nine. The story of Joe Louis and Max Schmeling started as one about "good versus evil" and "hero versus villain," but ended as a tale of two friends who looked past all the propaganda, politics, and hard punches . . . and saw each other as people.

J. R. R. Tolkien
C. S. Lewis

« CHAPTER 9 »

C. S. LEWIS

&

J. R. R. TOLKIEN

THE FELLOWSHIP OF THE INKLINGS

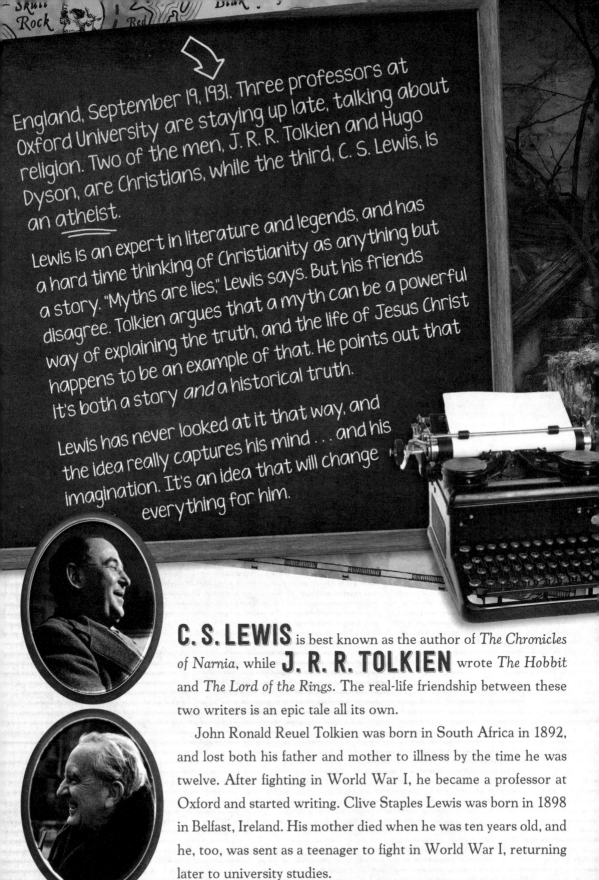

England, September 19, 1931. Three professors at Oxford University are staying up late, talking about religion. Two of the men, J. R. R. Tolkien and Hugo Dyson, are Christians, while the third, C. S. Lewis, is an atheist.

Lewis is an expert in literature and legends, and has a hard time thinking of Christianity as anything but a story. "Myths are lies," Lewis says. But his friends disagree. Tolkien argues that a myth can be a powerful way of explaining the truth, and the life of Jesus Christ happens to be an example of that. He points out that it's both a story *and* a historical truth.

Lewis has never looked at it that way, and the idea really captures his mind . . . and his imagination. It's an idea that will change everything for him.

C. S. LEWIS is best known as the author of *The Chronicles of Narnia*, while **J. R. R. TOLKIEN** wrote *The Hobbit* and *The Lord of the Rings*. The real-life friendship between these two writers is an epic tale all its own.

John Ronald Reuel Tolkien was born in South Africa in 1892, and lost both his father and mother to illness by the time he was twelve. After fighting in World War I, he became a professor at Oxford and started writing. Clive Staples Lewis was born in 1898 in Belfast, Ireland. His mother died when he was ten years old, and he, too, was sent as a teenager to fight in World War I, returning later to university studies.

TOLKIEN PROBABLY WOULD HAVE FELT AT HOME IN THIS HOBBIT DWELLING.

Tolkien and Lewis first met as professors at Oxford in 1926 and quickly became friends, connecting over their shared passions and experiences. They'd each lost parents at a young age and witnessed the horrors of war. Maybe this was why they both loved ancient heroic tales and fantastic stories of fictional kingdoms over grief-filled reality. But most of these myths, like *Beowulf* or the Norse stories of Asgard, had been created hundreds of years ago. Why wasn't anybody writing new ones? And why were the old ones thought of as being only for children? "If they won't write the kinds of books we want to read," Lewis told Tolkien, "we shall have to write them ourselves."

This idea inspired them to form the Inklings, a casual club of mostly Oxford professors dedicated to writing and sharing stories of fantasy and science fiction. Starting around 1930, a dozen or so writers would meet every Thursday in a pub or in Lewis's or Tolkien's rooms at the university. They ate and drank, and read their new material out loud for the group to discuss. Here, Tolkien first developed the world of Middle Earth,

OXFORD: A SETTING TO INSPIRE FANTASY

the home of elves, hobbits, wizards, and orcs. He was sometimes reluctant to share his writing, and not all the Inklings liked it. Hugo Dyson, a Shakespeare expert, sometimes shouted, "No more elves!" in response to another night of Tolkien's tales.

Lewis, however, loved Tolkien's stories and strongly encouraged his friend to publish them. It was exactly what Tolkien needed to keep writing. If Lewis hadn't wanted to hear more, Tolkien's bestselling books like *The Hobbit* and *The Lord of the Rings* might still be unfinished stories. "He was for long my only audience," Tolkien wrote of Lewis. "Only from him did I ever get the idea that my 'stuff' could be more than a private hobby."

Lewis was also creating stories, thanks in part to Tolkien's efforts to lead him back to Christianity. His newfound faith inspired Lewis to write, and he put his beliefs into nearly everything he published. *The Chronicles of Narnia* is set in a world of witches, monsters, and talking animals, but it's also filled with Christian symbolism and themes.

Things between these two friends weren't totally equal, though. Tolkien rarely gave Lewis the kind of support and praise that Lewis had shown him. He thought Lewis wrote and published too quickly: The seven Narnia books came out in seven years, while Tolkien spent twelve years on *The Lord of the Rings* alone. Tolkien also wasn't a fan of the obvious Christian imagery in Lewis's books. He preferred to keep themes and symbolism buried deeper in the writing so they didn't pull the reader away from the story.

In a clear sign that Tolkien and Lewis were growing apart, the Inklings had stopped holding meetings by the start of 1950. Tolkien was working intensely to finish *The Lord of the Rings* in the late 1940s, and that may have left him with no time for his friends. His obvious dislike for *The Lion, the Witch and the Wardrobe*, which Lewis completed in 1949, probably didn't help.

But the growing coldness between the two men was about more than just their writing. Tolkien had been overjoyed to help Lewis find religion, but was deeply disappointed when Lewis became a Protestant Anglican instead of a Catholic. Tolkien was also private and reserved, keeping a small circle of friends, while Lewis was more social and outgoing. When Lewis made new friends, or started spending lots of time with his wife, Tolkien may have felt left out. At the same time, Lewis may have felt equally abandoned when Tolkien no longer wanted or needed his feedback and encouragement to complete his books. In spite of this, Lewis remained an outspoken fan of his old friend's work. When the third volume of *The Lord of the Rings* came out in 1955, he wrote a glowing review, predicting: "I have little doubt that the book will soon take its place among the indispensables." He was right.

C. S. Lewis died in 1963. His seven-book Narnia series was already on its way to becoming a bestselling classic of children's literature. By the time J. R. R. Tolkien

Sci-Fi Guys

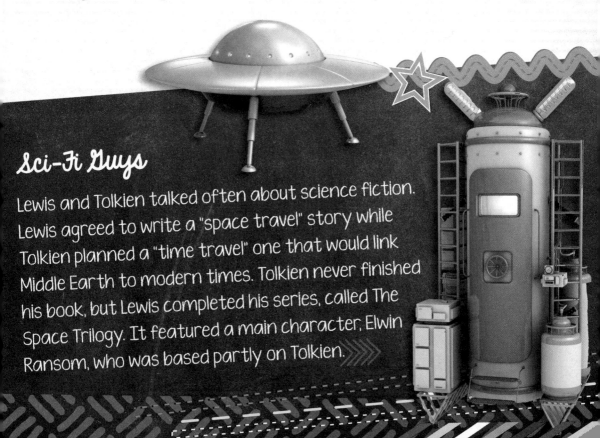

Lewis and Tolkien talked often about science fiction. Lewis agreed to write a "space travel" story while Tolkien planned a "time travel" one that would link Middle Earth to modern times. Tolkien never finished his book, but Lewis completed his series, called The Space Trilogy. It featured a main character, Elwin Ransom, who was based partly on Tolkien.

Magic at the Movies

Even though they don't really exist, Narnia and Middle Earth are permanently on the map of pop culture. The first three films based on the Narnia books have earned over $1.5 billion worldwide. Meanwhile, the six films based on *The Hobbit* and *The Lord of the Rings* have, by some estimates, brought in more than $5 billion, turning Tolkien's works into one of the most successful movie franchises of all time.

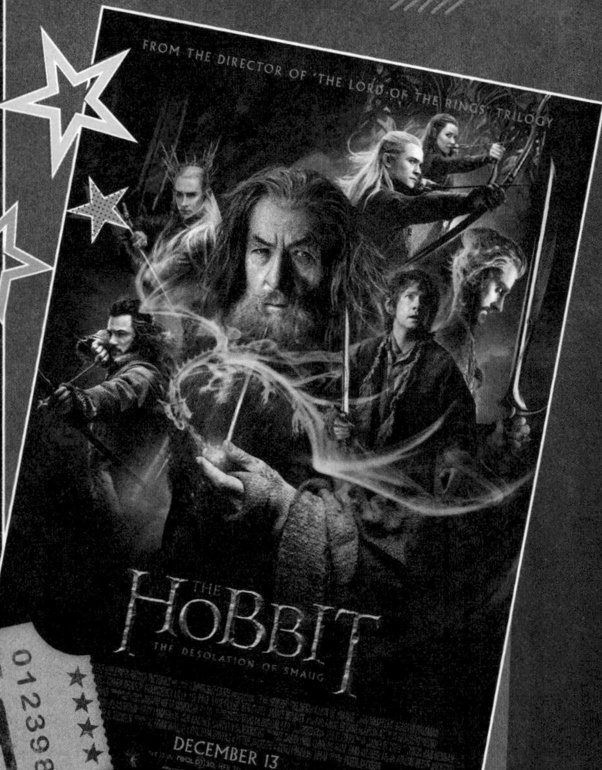

passed away in 1973, his novels were among the best-loved books in the world, selling millions of copies. He was a bona fide celebrity, but he hated the attention and chose a quiet retirement, working on tales of Middle Earth to the end. In his last years, he relied on his son Christopher Tolkien for the support he'd once gotten from Lewis. He wrote that when friends died it made him feel "like an old tree that is losing all its leaves one by one." To him, Lewis's death felt "like an axe-blow near the roots."

Clearly, their friendship was never entirely gone. It was just buried beneath the surface, like the roots of a tree.

Today, countless readers enjoy *The Chronicles of Narnia* as children, then go on to discover the more "grown-up" fantasy of *The Lord of the Rings*. The two works of literature become companions . . . just as their authors once were.

Ella Fitzgerald
Marilyn Monroe

« CHAPTER 10 »

Ella FITZGERALD & Marilyn MONROE

CELEBRITY SISTERHOOD

Hollywood, California, 1955. The Mocambo nightclub is *the* hotspot for anyone who's rich, famous, or both. If you're a performer, playing on the Mocambo stage means hitting the big time, but the owner, a man named Charlie Morrison, has to believe you're exciting enough to belong there.

Ella Fitzgerald is a popular African American jazz singer with several hit records. The Mocambo would take her to the next level, but even though black artists have headlined there before, Morrison refuses to book her because he doesn't think Ella—or the jazz she sings—is glamorous enough for his club.

Then one day, Morrison gets a phone call. On the other end of the line is someone so glamorous, her photo could appear under that word in the dictionary. It's mega movie star Marilyn Monroe.

Marilyn has a favor to ask, and it's one that will change Ella's life . . .

Doing something really cool for someone you don't know well can be the start of a great friendship, even between two people who seem as different as **ELLA FITZGERALD** and **MARILYN MONROE**.

Born in 1917, Ella Fitzgerald grew up in Yonkers, New York, with her mother and stepfather. The family struggled financially, and to help, Ella took on small jobs, including delivering money for local gamblers. It wasn't exactly a storybook childhood, but she got good grades, made friends, and loved to dance and sing.

Things changed drastically when her mother died when Ella was just fifteen. She went to live with an aunt but started skipping school. When Ella found herself in trouble with the police, she was sent first to an orphanage and then to a reform school.

MARILYN: ALWAYS IN THE SPOTLIGHT

Reform school must have been as terrible as it sounds, because Ella ran away. She lived on the street for a while, broke and alone, but held on to her dream of performing. One day, her name was pulled in a weekly drawing to compete in Amateur Night at the famed Apollo Theater in Harlem. The homeless teen sang, amazed the audience, and won the twenty-five-dollar prize. A musician in the audience recognized Ella's star potential and helped her get a job singing in a band. From there, her career took off.

When she wasn't onstage or around familiar people, Ella was quiet and shy. She was also self-conscious about her appearance. Once she started singing, though, her fears fell away. "I felt the acceptance and love from my audience," Ella once said. The girl with the rough start had finally found her home in the spotlight, and when she was twenty-one, she had her first number-one single.

In Los Angeles, California, a little girl named Norma Jeane Mortenson, who was born in 1926, was also doing her best to survive a crummy childhood. Her mother

The city of bright lights and big dreams.

suffered from serious mental illness and was in and out of psychiatric hospitals, so Norma Jeane spent her early years living with foster families, in an orphanage, and with family friends. One way she escaped the challenges of real life was through movies, and Norma Jeane dreamed of becoming an actress. Eager to change her life, she married her boyfriend, Jimmy Dougherty, when she was just sixteen.

When her new husband was sent overseas to fight in World War II, Norma Jeane went to work at a factory. There, she was discovered by a photographer who helped her launch a modeling career. A few years later, Norma Jeane, now divorced from Jimmy, jumped into acting with a film studio contract, a head of dyed platinum-blonde hair, and a new name: Marilyn Monroe. By 1953, she'd gone from playing small roles to starring in hit movies as one of the biggest names in Hollywood.

Marilyn built a career out of playing seductive "dumb blonde" characters, but that was all an act. (She was an actress, after all.) Offscreen, Marilyn loved to read and was eager to improve herself in every way. She wanted to become a better singer for musical roles, so a friend gave her Ella Fitzgerald's album *Ella Sings Gershwin*. Marilyn listened to it often, learning from Ella's unique sound, and quickly became a superfan.

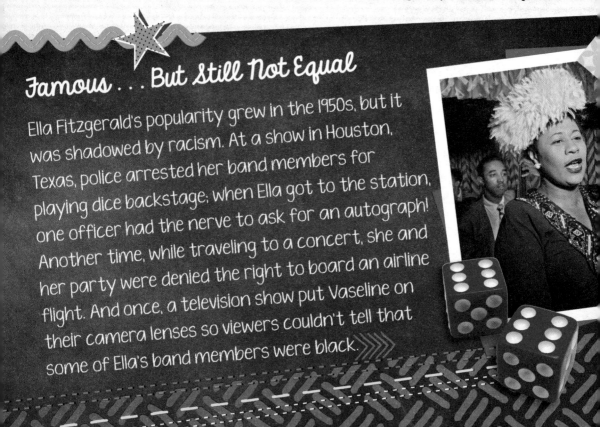

Famous . . . But Still Not Equal

Ella Fitzgerald's popularity grew in the 1950s, but it was shadowed by racism. At a show in Houston, Texas, police arrested her band members for playing dice backstage; when Ella got to the station, one officer had the nerve to ask for an autograph! Another time, while traveling to a concert, she and her party were denied the right to board an airline flight. And once, a television show put Vaseline on their camera lenses so viewers couldn't tell that some of Ella's band members were black.

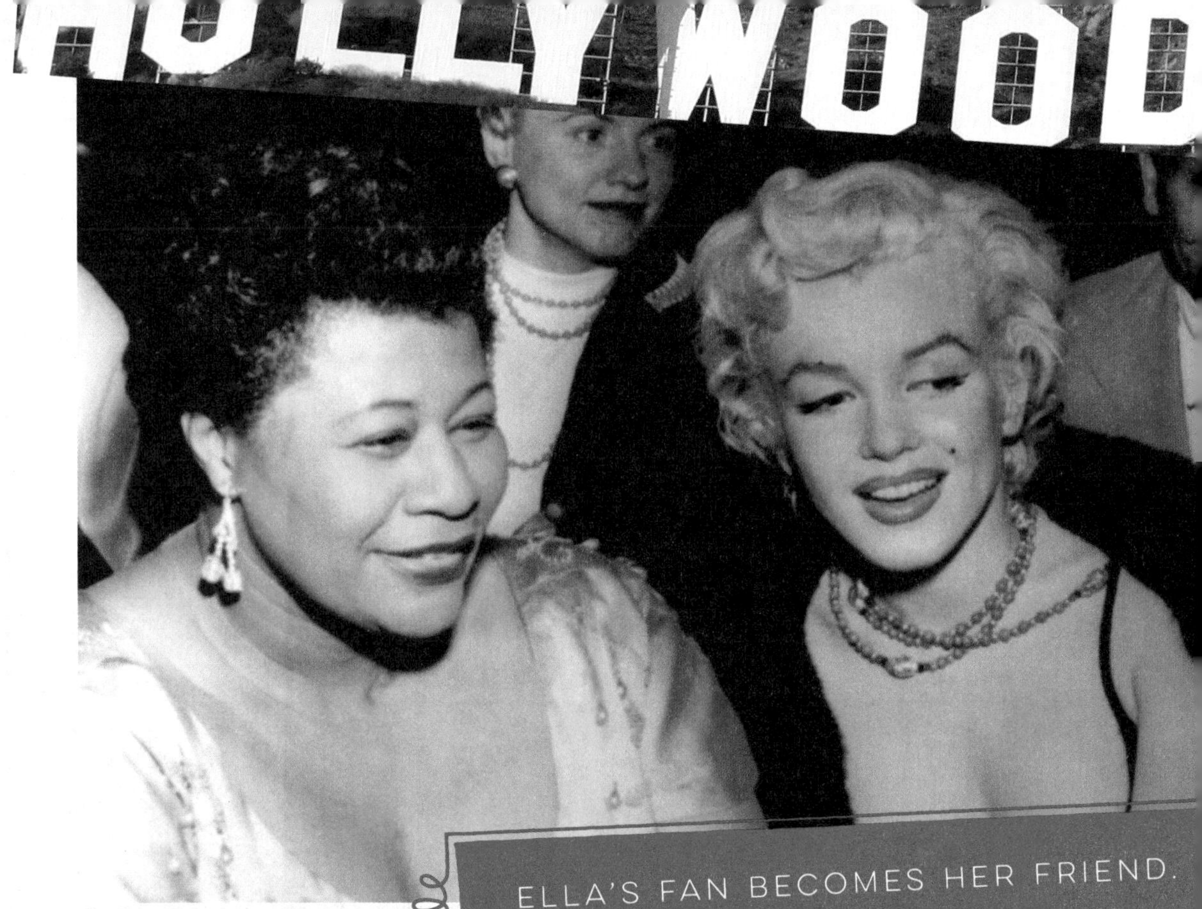

ELLA'S FAN BECOMES HER FRIEND.

Millions idolized Marilyn, and Marilyn idolized Ella. Finally, she got the chance to meet the singer she adored. A photo taken in November 1954 at the Tiffany Club in Hollywood shows the pair together, talking and laughing like BFFs. Maybe they clicked over their similar childhood experiences. Each woman had overcome gigantic obstacles to make her dreams come true, and each tapped into her tough background to give depth to her performances. Both women had to deal with people making assumptions about them based on their appearances, especially Ella, who faced racism in many of the places she toured.

Not long after, Marilyn made that call to Charlie Morrison at the Mocambo. Ella remembered how it went:

"She told him she wanted me booked immediately, and if he would do it, she would take a front table every night. She told him—and it was true, due to Marilyn's superstar status—that the press would go wild."

The Mocambo couldn't say no to a star like Marilyn, and Ella took their stage by storm. "After that," she said, "I never had to play a small jazz club again."

Marilyn soon had some life-altering experiences herself. She formed her own film production company and moved to New York to study theater at the legendary Actor's Studio. "I want good stories and good directors," she once said. "I am a serious actress. I want to prove it."

Ella remembered this about Marilyn: "She was an unusual woman—a little ahead of her times. And she didn't know it." In the years that followed, Marilyn and Ella remained friends, with Marilyn often traveling to see Ella perform in concert.

Ella quickly sealed her reputation as "The First Lady of Song" and a pioneer of "scat" singing (a typically improvised style that uses wordless notes or nonsense syllables like "do-wah"). She was one of the first jazz singers to cross over into pop music.

MARILYN AND ELLA: SUPERSTARS OF SHOWBIZ

More Than Just a Pretty Face

Like her acting, Marilyn Monroe's singing was much better than some people give her credit for. She studied with a vocal coach throughout her career and eventually mastered many different styles. "I won't be satisfied until people want to hear me sing without looking at me," she once said. When she sang her famous sultry rendition of "Happy Birthday, Mr. President" to John F. Kennedy in 1962, she was basically making fun of her blonde-bombshell image.

Marilyn's impact was also huge. She helped create the idea of a star as a style icon; instead of following trends, she started her own. Any time you see a celebrity with super-blonde hair and bright red lipstick, that's proof of her lasting power.

Many people know how Marilyn's story tragically ended: In August 1965, when she was just thirty-six, she was found dead of a drug overdose—an apparent suicide. Ella, meanwhile, went on to live a long life. She continued to inspire young performers for decades to come and died in July 1996, at age seventy-nine.

Some friendships build slowly and steadily, while others are cemented by a single, important moment in time. Marilyn Monroe and Ella Fitzgerald may not have been besties, but their connection was still meaningful . . . and helped each woman leave an enormous mark on the entertainment world.

Paul McCartney
George Harrison
Ringo Starr
John Lennon
THE BEATLES
PARLOPHONE
THE BEATLES

CHAPTER 11

John LENNON

&

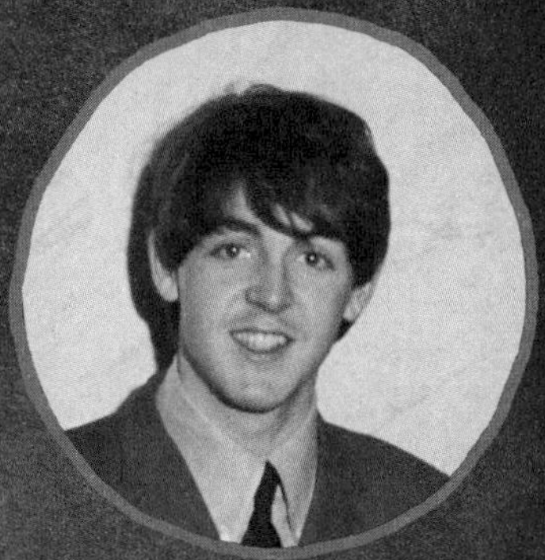

Paul MCCARTNEY

ALL YOU NEED IS LOVE

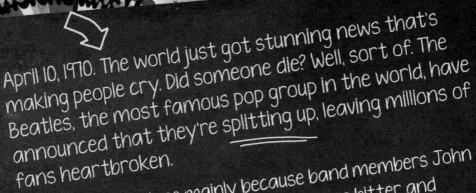

April 10, 1970. The world just got stunning news that's making people cry. Did someone die? Well, sort of. The Beatles, the most famous pop group in the world, have announced that they're splitting up, leaving millions of fans heartbroken.

The Beatles are done mainly because band members John Lennon and Paul McCartney have grown so bitter and angry toward each other, they're barely speaking. In a low blow, Paul announced the breakup at a press conference promoting his first record as a solo artist.

One of the saddest things about this day is not the end of the band but, rather, the end of a friendship between two young men who've been more like brothers than buddies for over a decade.

JOHN LENNON and **PAUL MCCARTNEY** first met on July 6, 1957, at a church fair in a suburb of their hometown of Liverpool, England, where John was playing with his band the Quarrymen. John was sixteen, and Paul had just turned fifteen. Paul saw John performing an American rock 'n' roll song and was impressed that, even though John didn't know all the words, he could make up new ones that fit. John was equally impressed with Paul's skills on the piano and that he knew how to tune a guitar properly (John had been tuning his like a banjo). John instantly wanted Paul to join the Quarrymen, but worried that Paul was so good he might overshadow him as band leader. He asked him anyway, and Paul accepted. From that point on, at least in terms of music, the boys saw themselves as equals.

BEATLES FOR SALE!

On the surface, the two teens seemed very different. John was a loud, outspoken troublemaker, while Paul was quieter, all smiles and charm. But these contrasting qualities actually helped them connect. John was hard on the outside but thoughtful and warm once Paul got to know him. Paul was the opposite: easygoing to strangers but sometimes tough on his close friends.

The boys also had a lot in common. Both were funny, smart, and interested in books and art. They loved drawing funny cartoons—the weirder the better. More importantly, they shared an obsession with American movies and music, especially rock 'n' roll performers like Elvis Presley and Buddy Holly.

When John was seventeen, his mother, Julia, was killed when a car struck her. The boys now sadly had this in common, too: Paul's mother had died of cancer a few years earlier. Paul later said that these losses, and the fact that they had to deal with intense emotions while still so young, were a big part of their connection.

FOUR LADS FROM LIVERPOOL, ABOUT TO HIT THE BIG TIME

The teens began to spend a ton of time together at Paul's house, dreaming up original rock tunes as the songwriting team of Lennon and McCartney. Writing songs was almost like a competition, with each trying to come up with better chords and lyrics until the final product was as good as it could be. John once said that Paul provided the "lightness and optimism" in a song while he would always "go for the sadness." They pushed each other in the best of ways.

By the end of 1960, the band, now called the Beatles and including guitarist George Harrison and drummer Pete Best, had found work in Hamburg, Germany. They played hundreds of shows in seedy nightclubs and bars, and the long hours made them into stronger musicians and performers. The four guys slept on bunk beds in a tiny room behind a movie theater, and this time together cemented the brotherly bond between John and Paul.

In 1962, the Beatles replaced Pete Best with drummer Ringo Starr and began making records in London. Thanks in part to tireless promotion by their manager, Brian Epstein, their singles quickly started topping the British charts. Hit records led to sold-out concerts, and the Beatles soon became a worldwide sensation. They toured the globe, made endless TV and radio appearances, and starred in movies. Their faces were in nearly every teen and music magazine, and fans lined up to buy Beatle wigs, Beatle dolls, and even Beatle bedsheets. Their music and personalities drove people, mostly teenage girls, into frenzies. It was a hurricane called "Beatlemania," and the "Fab Four" from Liverpool were the most famous people on the planet.

By the summer of 1963, the Beatles were usually one of three places: onstage, in a limousine, or in a hotel room. Going out in public was nearly impossible, because screaming fans chased them wherever they went. Once again, John and Paul were almost never apart. Trapped in hotels with nothing else to do, they improved as songwriters, and the success of their songs made them even richer and more famous. As a symbol of their friendship, they had agreed long ago to stick with Lennon/McCartney as the writing credit on all their compositions, even if only one of them had done the writing.

But Beatlemania didn't last. By 1966, life as a touring Beatle was so exhausting that George Harrison was thinking about quitting the group. The other Beatles felt the same, and the four decided they would stop touring and only make records. Most people agree that this is when the Beatles became truly great musicians, with long nights in the recording studio replacing months on tour. But with more time to spend apart in London, they also gradually stopped being Beatles and grew into individuals. John and Paul almost never wrote songs face-to-face anymore; instead, they'd write separately and bring their ideas to the studio. They started to develop different circles of friends, too. By the late 1960s, the Beatles were more like coworkers than brothers, and going to the recording studio was kind of like showing up to a job. The records kept getting better, but the friendships were drifting apart.

In 1967, after the death of Brian Epstein, the Beatles formed a company called Apple Corps to manage their money themselves. They soon discovered the job was much harder than it seemed, and the difficulty of being businessmen led to lots of bickering. In the studio, they were still recording Beatles records,

From Darkness to Light

Why did the Beatles become so popular in America so quickly? Many historians point to the assassination of President John F. Kennedy in November 1963, which shocked the nation into a mood of sadness and gloom. When these energetic and attractive lads arrived from England three months later, they brought just the sort of positive distraction that young Americans needed to feel good again.

but often worked on them alone. "John songs" and "Paul songs" began to sound very different from each other, just as the two friends were separating in real life.

At the start of 1969, the Beatles were falling apart. The recording sessions for their new album were miserable, with the four mates sulking, arguing, and occasionally walking out. John was more interested in spending time with his new artist friend Yoko Ono than with Paul, and when John brought Yoko into the recording studio, it created tension and resentment.

On March 12, 1969, Paul McCartney married Linda Eastman, an American photographer. Eight days later, John Lennon, now divorced from his first wife, Cynthia, married Yoko Ono. With new wives, the two old friends had less time for each other and more interests outside of the band. In September 1969, John told the other Beatles that he wanted out of the group. Paul reacted by leaving for his farm in Scotland with Linda, becoming depressed, and writing songs for his solo album. It was like the two men were going through their own divorce, ending a deep friendship of twelve years. In April of the following year, Paul made news of the split public.

AS THEIR FAME INCREASED, SO DID THE PRESSURE TO KEEP PRODUCING HITS

Pop and Popularity

Although the Beatles parted ways in 1970, their brand has never been more valuable. Fans have bought more than two billion copies of their albums, and a greatest hits CD released in 2000 became the bestselling album of that entire decade. More products featuring the Beatles logo or faces are available now than when they were still ecording, including clothing, games, artwork, housewares, toys, and even an e cream flavor created in honor of John Lennon. The rights to the Lennon/ lcCartney songs alone are worth a reported two billion dollars.

John Lennon and Paul McCartney stayed angry at each other throughout the early 1970s. They almost never spoke, and each released songs that contained nasty messages to the other. But by the middle of the decade, their anger had cooled, and they would visit each other when their busy schedules allowed. In March 1974, they had a jam session at a Los Angeles recording studio, playing the old rock 'n' roll songs they'd loved as teenagers. "We had a pretty difficult time," John said about their split. "But now, we're pretty close."

They would never re-create that brotherly bond they shared in the 1960s, but they'd dealt with their differences and figured out how to be friends again. Perhaps time apart, growing into themselves—and growing up—had made it easier to see the important things. Paul said years later that the breakup was not what mattered in the end; what mattered was the affection between them.

On December 8, 1980, John Lennon was shot and killed by a mentally ill fan. In a moment of senseless violence, the world lost a great musician and artist. Yoko lost a husband, and John's two sons lost a father. Paul McCartney lost the man who'd once been his closest friend. Without each other, John's and Paul's lives, and in many ways the future of music, would have been very different. They're proof that some friendships, though they can be intense and full of drama, are worth fighting for in the end.

Chris Evert
Martina Navratilova

« CHAPTER 12 »

Chris EVERT

&

Martina NAVRATILOVA

COMPETITIVE COMPADRES

July 1978. A young woman named Martina Navratilova is *this* close to making her dream come true.

She's the number-two female tennis player in the world, but she's never won a Grand Slam tournament. Today, she's facing off against the number-one-ranked Chris Evert in the Wimbledon championship. It's a tough match. Both players are so good. They fight ruthlessly for every single point.

But Martina fights a little harder, plays a little better, and eventually hits that final winning shot. She jumps for joy, then rushes to hug one of her closest friends, the person who understands better than anyone how much this victory means.

It's the same person who just tried to beat her.

MARTINA NAVRATILOVA versus **CHRIS EVERT** is one of the longest and most intense rivalries between any two athletes in sports history. Over the course of fifteen years, they played each other *eighty* times! Sixty of those were finals, with fourteen Grand Slam finals (the four biggest tournaments in tennis: Wimbledon, the US Open, the Australian Open, and the French Open).

Behind that rivalry was an amazing friendship fueled by competition.

Chris Evert was born in 1954 and grew up in Fort Lauderdale, Florida, learning tennis from her father and becoming one of the best teen players in America. When she exploded onto the professional tennis scene at age sixteen, fans and the media embraced her as the Next Big Thing.

QUEENS OF THE COURT

Martina Navratilova was born in 1956 in Czechoslovakia (now the Czech Republic), a Communist country where personal opportunities and freedom were extremely limited. As a teen tennis player, she admired Chris Evert and everything Martina felt she represented about American athletes: poise, ability, and sportsmanship. Martina dreamed of getting to play against Chris, and it kept her motivated to improve.

When Chris and Martina did start facing each other in competitions, Chris almost always won. The public saw them as total opposites. Martina's playing style was to serve and then run close to the net, while Chris usually stayed at the back of the court. With her lace tennis dresses and ponytails tied with ribbons, Chris looked sweet and soft on the outside. But inside, she was tough: She never broke down or burst out even during the most nail-biting matches. Martina had the hard exterior—she was tall and muscular, and from a country many Americans saw as a political enemy at the time—but often cried or lost her cool on the court.

But off the court, they found common ground.

Traveling the world from one tennis event to the next, they were frequently in the same place at the same time. "I used to tell her about all my problems with boyfriends," Chris said, "and we really got to know and care about each other." Martina remembered: "I used to turn to Chris a lot for help and advice in those early years in America, and she was always so understanding."

Before a big match against each other, they would practice together, have lunch, then go out and play their final. When one would hit a point-winning shot, the other sometimes muttered, "Too good!" Eventually, one of them would win, they'd shake hands at the net, and fly to the next city together. The pair grew so close that Chris invited Martina to play doubles with her, and they won two Grand Slam titles as a team.

Now Chris, whom Martina had always looked up to, returned those feelings of respect. "I would wonder why she couldn't control herself in front of sixty million people on TV," said Chris about Martina. But she also admired how Martina was able to let her emotions out and secretly wished she could do the same. At age eighteen, Martina defected to the United States, renouncing her Czech citizenship and declaring her intention to become an American citizen. It meant Martina might never see her family again, and Chris was in awe of this brave, risky move.

You Go, Girl!

The 1970s were an important decade for women's sports. A few of the highlights: Richard Nixon signed the Title IX law that gave girls equal access to many school athletic programs; Nadia Comaneci of Romania became the first Olympic gymnast to score a perfect 10; and American Janet Guthrie was the first woman to compete in the Indianapolis 500.

MARTINA WINS AT WIMBLEDON . . . ONE OF A RECORD NINE TIMES!

Not long after, something changed. Since they'd first met, Chris had always been the one on top, beating Martina in most of their matches. When Martina started to win more often, Chris felt threatened. She thought that Martina knew her game too well since they were always practicing together. She dumped their doubles partnership to focus on her singles career and get back to crushing her friend on the court again.

Their relationship survived all the competition, and when Martina won that first big final at Wimbledon in 1978, the hug they shared was between real friends.

Sticks and Stones

Both Chris and Martina got stuck with some not-so-nice nicknames from the press. They called Martina "The Great Wide Hope" (when she gained weight from eating American food) and "Navrat the Brat," while Chris was known as "The Ice Maiden."

Then came another shift. Martina had new advisers who told her that if she wanted to be the best, she would have to distance herself from Chris. She took their suggestion, trained hard, and won thirteen matches in a row against her friend. The media began portraying their rivalry as "Martina the Villain from a Communist Country" versus "Chris the All-American Girl Next Door."

Despite the media pressure, the two friends still cared deeply about each other. When Martina went public with the fact that she was gay, Chris supported her. After Martina beat Chris in the Australian Open, Chris broke down in the locker room, and her friend was there to comfort her. Martina knew exactly what that kind of frustration and disappointment felt like.

Martina's new winning streak motivated Chris to train differently. After thirteen losses, she finally won again. It was an extra-sweet victory for Chris because she was older. She'd been thinking about retiring, but facing off against Martina had kept her in the game. "The rivalry made us both better players," said Martina. That rivalry also gave a huge boost to women's sports at a time when people were starting to take female athletes seriously, and when culture and politics were focusing more on women's equality in general.

In 1986, Martina finally had the chance to go home. She'd been chosen as captain of a US women's tennis team (with Chris as a teammate) that would compete in Prague, the Czech capital. As the Czech national anthem played during the opening ceremonies, Martina began to cry, and Chris reached out and comforted her. On their day off, Martina took Chris (and teammate Pam Shriver) to her hometown, where Martina's mother cooked dumplings for them. "That was one of the all-time great days for me," said Martina. She was thrilled to have Chris share it with her.

Shortly after that, Martina invited Chris on a ski trip and introduced her to Andy Mill, a former US Olympic skier. Chris and Andy hit it off so well that they ended up getting married and having three children. (Martina was a guest at the wedding, of course.)

In the end, Martina grabbed the edge from Chris in their overall statistics—she won forty-three of their eighty matches, while Chris won thirty-seven—but their friendship continued long after they both retired. When Martina married her long-time partner, Julia Lemigova, in 2014, Chris was one of her matrons of honor.

Martina once told Chris, "There are three or four people I can call at any time and I always knew you would be one of those people . . . It doesn't matter if we don't see each other for a week or for a year, it's like we just saw each other yesterday."

For Chris and Martina, rivalry and friendship were two halves of an extraordinary connection that helped two talented women achieve their dreams.

FIERCE RIVALS, LOYAL FRIENDS

Alex Rodriguez
Derek Jeter

« CHAPTER 13 »

Derek JETER

&

Alex RODRIGUEZ

FROM BEST BUDS TO BAD BLOOD

April 2001. Twenty-five-year-old baseball shortstop Alex "A-Rod" Rodriguez is making waves . . . and not the fun kind that fans do in the stands.

He'd recently become the highest paid athlete in US history when the Texas Rangers agreed to pay him $252 million over ten years to play on their team. That meant each time he went up to bat, he'd be earning more money than an average American makes in a year! Many people wondered if he was worth it.

Now A-Rod has just trash-talked New York Yankees shortstop Derek Jeter in a magazine interview. "Jeter's been blessed with great talent around him," he told the reporter. "He's never had to lead." It seemed like Rodriguez was hinting that Jeter had it easy because his teammates did all the hard work for him.

Rodriguez is disrespecting one of the most popular players in baseball, a star with four World Series rings (Rodriguez, meanwhile, has zero). What makes it worse is that everyone thought Rodriguez and Jeter were best friends. What exactly is A-Rod up to? And how will Jeter respond?

DEREK JETER was raised in New Jersey and Michigan. He grew up a Yankees fan, so it was a dream come true when the team drafted him in 1992, before Jeter had even turned eighteen. A year later, **ALEX RODRIGUEZ**, a high school senior from Florida who was expecting to be chosen by the Seattle Mariners, called Jeter up to ask about his experiences as a young first-round draft pick. That phone call led to many more, and it wasn't long before the two star players, both still teenagers, were best buds.

They had plenty in common. Just a year apart in age (Jeter was born in June 1974 and A-Rod in July 1975), both were handsome and charming. The two actually looked so much alike that in

HIGH FIVES IN HAPPIER TIMES

public, one was often mistaken for the other. They were equally awesome on the field: In 1996, Major League Baseball named Jeter Rookie of the Year, while two groups of sports writers chose Rodriguez as Player of the Year.

Inside the stadium they were rivals, but outside the gates, they were simply friends. When the Mariners played in New York, Rodriguez would stay at Jeter's apartment, and when the Yankees traveled to Seattle, A-Rod welcomed Jeter as his guest. They were often seen together in nightclubs and restaurants. Rodriguez said, "Derek has become like my brother."

During a Yankees-Mariners game in August 1999, tensions in the game exploded into a bench-clearing brawl. As the players threw punches, Rodriguez and Jeter approached each other and appeared to be talking as pals instead of fighting like everyone else. One of the Yankees later accused Jeter of being disloyal, but Rodriguez immediately jumped to his friend's defense, labeling Jeter "the ultimate team player."

Then came the 2001 interview, and Rodriguez's unexpected, nasty comments suggesting he was better than Jeter. The press jumped on the story, trying to play up the idea of two friends who were suddenly enemies. Some fans and journalists instantly cast A-Rod in the role of villain, calling him arrogant and jealous. In contrast, most people considered Jeter to be a humble, charitable, and generally great guy.

Speaking to reporters, Jeter tried to play the whole thing down. "He said his intentions weren't bad," he said of A-Rod. "He is a good friend of mine." But it was clear that Rodriguez's comments had hurt Jeter and driven a wedge between them.

In 2004, something forced the former best bros back into the spotlight: the Yankees acquired A-Rod. How would things go with these two superstars in the same dugout? Both players insisted they were still close, and that there were no hard feelings on or off

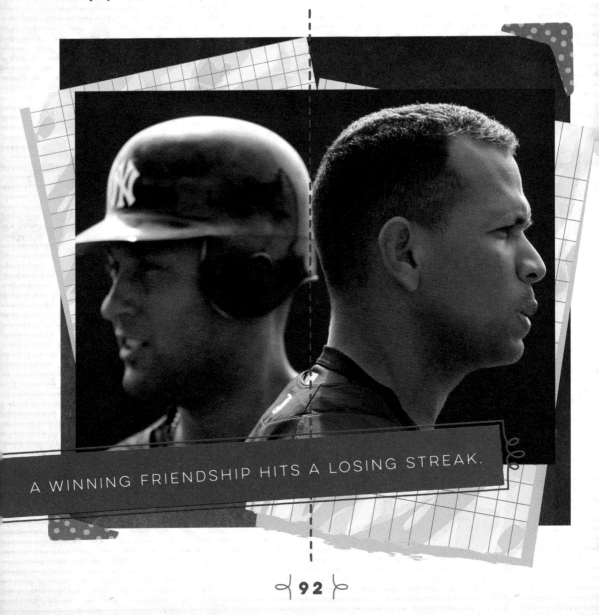

A WINNING FRIENDSHIP HITS A LOSING STREAK.

The M&M Boys

The most epic baseball bromance happened in 1961, when Yankees teammates Roger Maris and Mickey Mantle battled each other to beat Babe Ruth's single-season home run record of sixty. During that time, they kept up a close friendship and even shared an apartment. When Mantle got injured and had to quit the race, he cheered Maris on from his hospital room . . . until Maris finally hit that sixty-first homer into the history books.

the field. But others noticed a distance between them. It looked like an icy professional relationship instead of a warm and fuzzy bromance.

Rodriguez struggled through a tough 2006 season and the New York crowds booed him mercilessly. Jeter was team captain and a fan favorite, and some people thought he should do more to support his third baseman. "I can't tell the fans what to do," was all Jeter said . . . which didn't sound like much of a defense.

When Rodriguez was accused of using steroids (he later admitted this was true), Jeter's support also seemed halfhearted. Once during a game, the two collided and dropped a pop-fly ball, and fans thought they saw Jeter give Rodriguez a dirty look. A-Rod admitted in an interview that their friendship was essentially over. "There has been a change in our relationship in the last fourteen years," he said about Jeter. "Do we go to dinner every night like we used to? No."

For his part, Jeter told the press, "We support each other on the field and we want to win. That's the bottom line." It wasn't hard for fans to catch the drift. The two athletes were now teammates and nothing more.

A Yankee's First Contract

When Derek Jeter was growing up, his father, Charles, created a "good behavior contract" every year. Jeter was allowed to play baseball only if he signed it and followed all eighteen demands, which included strict bans on drinking, arguing, and disrespecting women.

In 2009, the Yankees won the World Series, thanks in part to great postseason performances by both Rodriguez and Jeter. It was A-Rod's first championship and Jeter's fifth. In the postgame clubhouse celebration, they hugged and smiled, pouring victory champagne over each other's heads. All that bad blood seemed to vanish in the joy of winning . . . unless it was just for the cameras.

VICTORY HEALS ALL WOUNDS . . . OR DOES IT?

Fast-forward five years: One player has found himself on top, while the other landed at the bottom: Derek Jeter's farewell season of 2014 was the same one Alex Rodriguez spent on the bench as punishment for his steroid use. That might have been a relief to Jeter, who'd grown tired of answering questions about his friendship with Rodriguez. Jeter could now have the spotlight all to himself in his final months as a Yankee.

Yet when Jeter and A-Rod crossed paths at a sports awards show in 2015, they ended up talking, smiling, and generally acting like old friends. The reporters started buzzing again. Was it real or just for show? Only the two of them know for sure.

Derek Jeter and Alex Rodriguez showed us the highs and lows of friendship in a fishbowl. The constant pressure of celebrity, competition, and the media didn't make things easy for this pair, but their story, and perhaps their friendship, too, is far from over.

FORMER BROS, BASEBALL LEGENDS

Patrick Stewart
Ian McKellen

CHAPTER 14

Ian MCKELLEN

&

Patrick STEWART

A FINE BROMANCE

March 2014. A pair of aging British guys are taking the Internet by storm.

The men are actors Ian McKellen and Patrick Stewart, and photos of them are being posted, shared, and favorited like crazy. People can't get enough of these pictures, which show the two men in matching black bowler hats, making funny faces, and striking weird poses in various New York City locations. In one shot, they're playing skeeball at Coney Island, and in another, they're pretending to be goofy tourists on the observation deck of the Empire State Building.

The photos, which are supposed to be a wacky way for Stewart and McKellen to promote a Broadway play they're performing in together, become an epic event of their own. Everyone loves the idea of these two distinguished actors—both of them famous for playing popular characters on TV and in film—being close buddies.

The best part is that all the fun and friendship in those photos is one-hundred percent real.

PATRICK STEWART and **IAN MCKELLEN** seemed like such naturals together, many people assumed they'd been BFFs for decades. But in reality, they didn't become close until pretty late in life.

Stewart was born in Yorkshire, England, in 1940. An elementary school English teacher changed his life by giving him a copy of a Shakespeare play and saying, "Now, get up on your feet and perform!" From that moment on, theater was his passion. When he lost all his hair at age nineteen, he grew self-conscious and timid, but acting helped him get past that.

Ian McKellen was born in 1939 in Lancashire, England, and spent many nights sleeping under the iron bomb-proof dining

JUST TWO PALS HAVING A BALL

table in his family's house as World War II raged outside. As he got older, his parents encouraged his interest in theater by bringing him to local performances. When McKellen won a scholarship to attend the prestigious University of Cambridge, he began acting in productions there.

Both men spent decades working steadily on stage and each performed with Britain's famous Royal Shakespeare Company at different times. Most of their work was serious and dramatic, but they both hit the big time with roles in science fiction and fantasy. Legions of fans love Stewart as Captain Picard from *Star Trek: The Next Generation*, and an equally powerful fandom adores McKellen as the wise wizard Gandalf from the multiple films based on *The Lord of the Rings* and *The Hobbit*.

"We are the same actor, really," McKellen joked once. "We've had the same career." Both men are even real-life knights—Queen Elizabeth II gave each of them that honor for their contributions to the performing arts.

Although they had met and knew each other casually, their paths didn't intersect too often. Since there aren't a lot of projects that need two of the same type of actor, McKellen and Stewart were often cast in similar roles but in different projects.

That all changed when they were both tapped to appear in the first *X-Men* film in 1999. With Stewart playing the noble Professor Xavier and McKellen cast as the evil mastermind Magneto, the two were enemies onscreen but became close friends behind the scenes. "It was movie making, so we spent more time sitting in our trailers than on the set," Stewart recalled. "We got to know one another and that's when the bond began."

McKellen remembered, "We fell into each other's arms because of our similarities in our career, and because of our age and because we like the same sort of things."

Better late than never: Stewart was fifty-nine at the time, and McKellen was sixty. They went on to do four more X-Men films together. As their real-life bromance took off, so did the relationship between their characters onscreen, with Professor X and Magneto evolving from enemies to frenemies.

In 2009, they had the chance to spend more time together where they both got their start: on the stage, in a British production of the play *Waiting for Godot* by

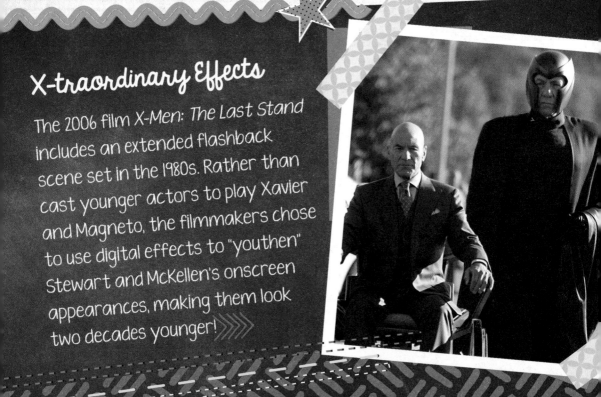

X-traordinary Effects

The 2006 film *X-Men: The Last Stand* includes an extended flashback scene set in the 1980s. Rather than cast younger actors to play Xavier and Magneto, the filmmakers chose to use digital effects to "youthen" Stewart and McKellen's onscreen appearances, making them look two decades younger!

STILL AWESOME AFTER ALL THESE YEARS

Samuel Beckett. The pals shared a dressing room and countless good times. After their final performance, McKellen broke down in tears, saying, "I despair if ever I'll enjoy myself as much again." They eventually agreed to do the play in New York, which inspired the photo shoot that made them the coolest duo on the Internet.

After the photos went viral, the actors decided to keep the fun rolling and took to social media to record dramatic readings of

These two sure are corn-y!

HELLO? IT'S ME . . . YOUR BEST BUD CALLING!

Taylor Swift songs. McKellen started off by reading "Bad Blood." Stewart responded with his version of "Blank Space," and then went online to ask Swift if he and McKellen could be part of her squad of famous friends (read more about Taylor's posse starting on page 105). The singer replied, "You've made my day. You two are ultimate squad goals."

Beyond the publicity stunts, Stewart and McKellen clearly have a real meaningful connection. Whenever they get the chance, the two knights are there for each other. McKellen was ordained as a minister so that he could officiate at his friend's 2013 wedding to musician Sunny Ozell. Two years later, Stewart showed up to the premiere of McKellen's latest movie, *Mr. Holmes*, where they shared a big hug (and even a kiss) in front of the cameras.

SERIOUS ACTORS? NOT ALWAYS . . .

For a variety of reasons, the camaraderie between Patrick Stewart and Ian McKellen makes people smile. Maybe it's the fun of seeing a spaceship captain being goofy with a wizard, or two mutant superheroes hanging out together IRL. Perhaps it's simply inspiring to see two older guys acting so young at heart.

Stewart and McKellen remind us that friendship soul mates can be found even late in life . . . and that whatever your age, it's a beautiful thing to be able to let loose, be silly, and show the world just how much fun you can have with a great BFF by your side.

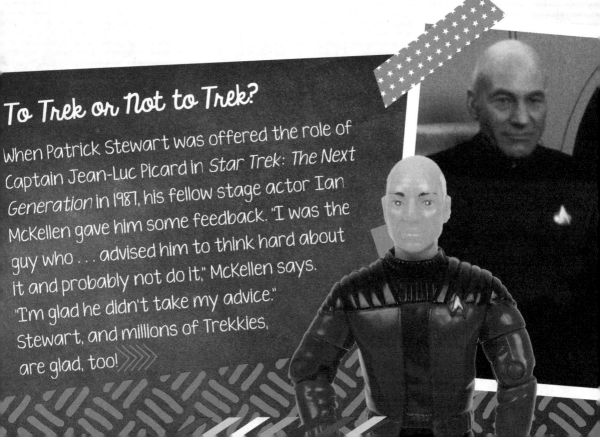

To Trek or Not to Trek?

When Patrick Stewart was offered the role of Captain Jean-Luc Picard in *Star Trek: The Next Generation* in 1987, his fellow stage actor Ian McKellen gave him some feedback. "I was the guy who . . . advised him to think hard about it and probably not do it," McKellen says. "I'm glad he didn't take my advice." Stewart, and millions of Trekkies, are glad, too!

Taylor Swift
Lorde
Selena Gomez

« CHAPTER 15 »

Taylor SWIFT

&

Her SQUAD

THE POWER OF A POSSE

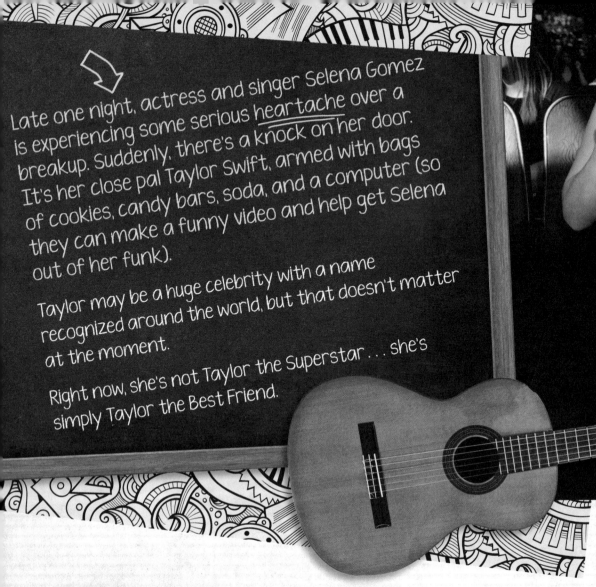

Late one night, actress and singer Selena Gomez is experiencing some serious heartache over a breakup. Suddenly, there's a knock on her door. It's her close pal Taylor Swift, armed with bags of cookies, candy bars, soda, and a computer (so they can make a funny video and help get Selena out of her funk).

Taylor may be a huge celebrity with a name recognized around the world, but that doesn't matter at the moment.

Right now, she's not Taylor the Superstar . . . she's simply Taylor the Best Friend.

TAYLOR SWIFT became famous for a lot of things. As in: releasing her first country music album, *Taylor Swift*, at age sixteen, then being the youngest artist ever to win an Album of the Year Grammy Award for her album *Fearless*, when she was just twenty years old. She's beloved by her fans for writing songs that tell great stories and capture hearts. She also became famous for something unexpected: dating one celebrity boyfriend after another (and recording songs about them). Then, when she was twenty-five, Taylor Swift started to become famous for something else: her famous friends.

In 2014, Taylor released her fifth album, titled *1989*. She was shifting from being a country music star to a true pop star,

PEACE SIGNS FOR THE PAPARAZZI

and she'd made a shift in her personal life, too. For years, her fans had seemed more interested in the singer's romantic relationships and the gossipy headlines than in her music. Taylor was sick of all that.

Instead, she started to focus on a different kind of relationship. She began surrounding herself with a squad of other young women she liked and admired . . . who all happened to be celebrities themselves.

Selena Gomez was already a bestie and Taylor's longest-running friendship. They met when they were both dating Jonas brothers. (Taylor was with Joe. Selena was with Nick.) When their respective romances flamed out, the girls kept their friendship burning bright. Whenever one was going through something rough, the other would hop on a plane to see her.

Also in the squad: New Zealand teenager and hit singer-songwriter Lorde. Before they met, Lorde gave an interview criticizing Taylor as "too flawless and unattainable," and may have seen Taylor as a rival. But Taylor simply saw a kindred spirit whose music she enjoyed. She sent Lorde flowers, congratulating her on her success—Taylor knew better than most people what it felt like to be young and have a quick rise to fame—and they arranged to meet up at a restaurant in New York City. It didn't take long before the two were often photographed attending award shows together and cheering each other on.

Taylor met model Karlie Kloss at a fashion show when they were introduced by a mutual friend who thought for sure they'd hit it off. That person was right, and Karlie and Taylor's friendship quickly grew so strong that Taylor set aside a special bedroom in her New York City apartment for Karlie to stay in when she was in town, filled with all her favorite snacks.

TAYLOR + LORDE = ONE MAJOR MUSICAL FRIENDSHIP

Pack Mentality

Taylor's squad is not the first group of celebrity friends to be recognized as a "thing," or even the first to have a name. In the 1950s and '60s, the crew known as the "Rat Pack" included actors Frank Sinatra, Dean Martin, and Sammy Davis Jr., who were all friends and appeared in several films together. More recently, actor George Clooney took a stab at creating a new version of the Rat Pack with buddies and co-stars Matt Damon, Brad Pitt, and others.

Other friends in Taylor's squad include actor-writer-director Lena Dunham, singer Ellie Goulding, and actresses Emma Stone and Hailee Steinfeld, just to name a few. Clearly, when you're someone like Taylor Swift and there's a person you want to be friends with, all you have to do is ask! (It's pretty likely she'll say yes.) Taylor once said in an interview: "When your number-one priority is getting a boyfriend, you're more inclined to see a beautiful girl and think, 'Oh, she's gonna get that hot guy I wish I was dating . . . But when you're not boyfriend shopping, you're able to step back and see other girls who are killing it and think, 'I want to be around her.'"

Instead of being photographed with her date-of-the-month, Taylor was now making headlines with one or more of her crew. She said, "It's the first time in my life that I've had anything strong like that in the friendship department." She'd often post personal photos of herself and her friends attending star-studded events, taking trips together, or simply hanging out by the pool or in the kitchen. During Taylor's live tour for *1989*, many of her pals appeared as surprise guests on stage. Her music video for the song

THE SWIFT SQUAD CELEBRATES ONSTAGE.

"Bad Blood" got a lot of attention because it was filled with cameos by Taylor's squad as well as women she looked up to as role models, all playing strong female action-hero characters.

With her gang of girlfriends, Taylor quickly transformed her former boy-crazy image into someone who'd grown up and found the confidence that can come from great female friendships, not romance. But was it real? Many fans wondered if Taylor was acting more like a "friend collector," trying to feel supported with a pool of celebs that was wide but not very deep. Did all these friends connect with one another, or were they only linked by Taylor? Were these true friendships or merely publicity stunts to get Taylor and her fellow stars into the spotlight?

Celebrity friendships certainly can't be easy. Because Taylor and her squad travel so much for their various jobs, in-person quality time must be hard to come by. And privacy? Impossible. Would it really be that fun to go shopping or get ice cream when you have bodyguards, paparazzi, and fans swarming around you?

Pop Star Pets

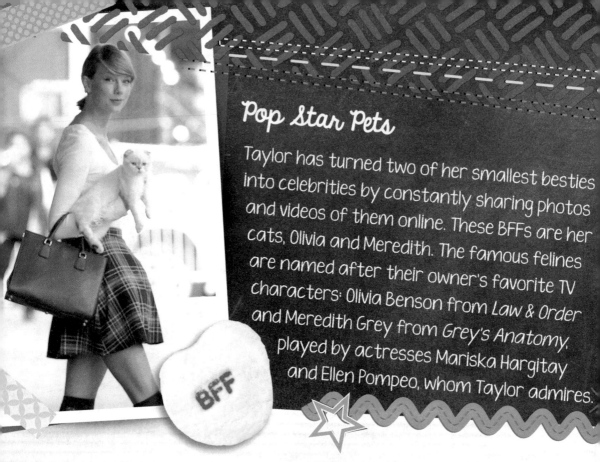

Taylor has turned two of her smallest besties into celebrities by constantly sharing photos and videos of them online. These BFFs are her cats, Olivia and Meredith. The famous felines are named after their owner's favorite TV characters: Olivia Benson from *Law & Order* and Meredith Grey from *Grey's Anatomy*, played by actresses Mariska Hargitay and Ellen Pompeo, whom Taylor admires.

Then again, hopping on a plane to deliver junk food and a shoulder to cry on for a friend in need is as much a sign of BFF love as anything. Setting up a guest bedroom in your house for one particular friend? That says *I care, for real*. These may seem over the top, but they're really just superstar versions of the small, daily gestures any pair of friends do for each other. Besides, no one else can really understand the pressures of fame like a fellow celebrity. In interviews, Taylor and her friends have described lots of group outings and private get-togethers. Maybe it's only with one another that these young stars can really be themselves and not feel judged.

Taylor Swift also knows about the pain and pitfalls of lost friendships. When "Bad Blood" was released, she said it was *not* about an ex-boyfriend but rather about a woman she'd thought was her friend. When fans went a little crazy trying to figure out exactly who that person was, Taylor made it clear that the point of the song was to express how friendships can break up, too, and those can hurt just as much as, and sometimes even more than, romantic breakups.

Selena, Lorde, Karlie, and the rest of Taylor's squad have showed everyone the value of a support network to stand by you and help you grow, make you laugh, and feel loved. Whether your crew is famous the world over or just rocking out in your room, true friendship is something to celebrate . . . many times over.